the MIRACLE MORNING
for Real Estate Agents

It's Your Time to Rise and Shine

Hal Elrod ⌂ Michael J. Maher
Michael Reese ⌂ Jay Kinder

with Honorée Corder

ISBN: 978-1-942589-00-6

Cover design by Hugo Fernandez and JD Media Productions
www.JDmediaProductions.com

Editing by Kandis Gaignard and Jaqueline Kyle

Interior layout by Christina Culbertson, 3CsBooks.com

WHAT TOP PRODUCERS & THOUGHT LEADERS ARE SAYING

"If you want to sell more homes and make more money, as fast as humanly possible, *The Miracle Morning for Real Estate Agents* is the one book that can take you there. The authors have already helped thousands of real estate agents achieve extraordinary success, and now it's your turn."
—**Pat Hiban, Former #1 RE/MAX® Agent, #1 Keller Williams® Realty Agent, and NY Times bestselling author,** *6 Steps to 7 Figures: A Real Estate Professional's Guide to Building Wealth and Creating Your Own Destiny*

"*The Miracle Morning for Real Estate Agents* will give you the gift of waking up each day to your full potential. It's time to stop putting off creating the life and business you've always wanted. This book will show you how."
—**Dr. Ivan Misner, CEO and Founder of BNI®**

"Seeing Hal Elrod and Michael Maher collaborate with Jay Kinder and Michael Reese is a real estate professional's dream come true! Whether you are a real estate agent or mortgage professional, if want to make more money in less time, I highly recommend that you pick up a copy of *The Miracle Morning for Real Estate Agents* today!"
—**Dan Keller, Mortgage Advisor, Host of** *Coffee With Keller,* **and voted "One of Seattle's Top Mortgage Professionals" by Seattle Magazine**

"*The Miracle Morning for Real Estate Agents* has become an incredibly important part of my life, and I love that I can customize it to fit my lifestyle. I love my silent time, my affirmations, my visualization, my exercise, and my reading. Love my Miracle Mornings!"
—**Diane Kink, GRI, ABR, ALC, Realtor®, CEO of** *The Kink Team,* **and one of the top Luxury Real Estate Agents in America**

"*The Miracle Morning for Real Estate Agents* is the best gift you can give to every agent and lender on your list. Hal Elrod's book, *The Miracle Morning*, has been one of the most important books that I've ever shared with friends and clients. Every time I share it with someone, they call me with a big thank you. Just be ready for the 'thank you' calls to start rolling in!"
—**Dave Savage, CEO of Mortgage Coach, and Co-founder at Real Estate Radio Network**

"*The Miracle Morning* and has been life and career-changing for me! I love how you can implement the lessons right away, with the great tips on how to make getting up early easier, and how to prevent hitting the snooze button over and over. Doing the most important things first every day gives me confidence and a great positive mindset. I've become healthier, and lost 50 pounds by sticking with the exercise part of the routine. Practicing the Miracle Morning, along with reading and following the business model in Michael Maher's *(7L) The Seven Levels of Communication*, has allowed me to grow my business by 145% this year! I've recommended *The Miracle Morning* and *(7L)* to my team members, clients, family, and anyone else who is seeking personal growth. Now I'll be recommending *The Miracle Morning for Real Estate Agents*!"
—**Cindy Carrigan, Team Leader, *Five Star Spokane Real Estate Group***

"Before *The Miracle Morning,* I woke up in the morning early to prospect; however, I had no real plan. Everything was sporadic and chaotic. Now, with *The Miracle Morning* and having taken the 30-Day Challenge, I have a plan and a system to be more productive in my business, and more importantly in life. So far, I have lost 22 pounds and on my way to losing 50. I get up every morning and workout as part of my Miracle Morning. I am more organized and am helping more people. I tell everyone I know about the 30-Day Challenge and have referred over 60 people so far. I truly believe that the Miracle Morning 30-Day Challenge is a way to change your destiny."
—**Dan Grieb, Team Leader, *The Dan Grieb Team* and founder of *The Elite REO Network***

"My first year of *The Miracle Morning* produced measurable results: personal income increased of over 29%, my fitness level is 15% better, aliveness, hope and confidence: up 30%. For me, *The Miracle Morning* is, and always has been, very personal. It is not a competition to see how many days in a row I can do or, a "have to" do it. It is a practice that has deepened my life. The compounded effect of my Miracle Morning is something, about which I am very excited, and my Miracle Morning practice is constantly evolving. It remains very personal, and I am grateful that it was written."
—**Lee Gallaher, Owner, Gallaher Real Estate**

"Michael J. Maher's *(7L) The Seven Levels of Communication* and Hal Elrod's *The Miracle Morning* are two of the most powerful and effective books that I have come across in terms of building a real estate career worth having and a life worth living. I was absolutely ECSTATIC when I saw that these two great/inspirational minds blended together to bring us *The Miracle Morning for Real Estate Agents*. The simple, yet powerfully effective lessons taught in this book are awaiting your implementation. This book is a legacy builder. Not only for the authors, but for each and every person that takes action on the wisdom within these pages."
—**Chad Hauer, Managing Broker,** *Hauer Real Estate Group*

"I never thought I would say this about a "morning book," but *The Miracle Morning CHANGED MY LIFE*. Yes, you've read that correctly. For years I've told myself "I'm not a morning person," and for the most part, it was true. In fact, one of my WHYs for wanting to be an entrepreneur was my desire to sleep in. No alarm clock. No getting up at dark. I wanted to wake up when I wanted to wake up. When I started reading this, I was curious to see if it could break my strong narrative and my strong why. It did. After reading this book I actually started getting up at 4:00 a.m. and hitting the gym. Yes, you've read the right. FOUR-FREAKING A.M. As a result, my days are far more productive and my physique is changing before my eyes. I never thought I could be one of these weirdos who gets up at 4AM. Now, I am one of those weirdos. I do it five times a week and mostly without an alarm clock."
—**MJ DeMarco, #1 Bestselling Author,** *The Millionaire Fastlane: Crack the Code to Wealth and Live Rich for a Lifetime*

A Special Invitation from Hal

Fans and readers of *The Miracle Morning* make up an extraordinary community of like-minded individuals who wake up each day dedicated to fulfilling the unlimited potential that is within all of us. As the author of *The Miracle Morning*, it was my desire to create an online space where readers and fans could go to connect, get encouragement, share best practices, support one another, discuss the book, post videos, find an accountability partner, and even swap smoothie recipes and exercise routines.

I honestly had no idea that The Miracle Morning Community would become one of the most inspiring, engaged, and supportive online communities in the world, but it has. I'm blown away by the caliber of our 40,000+ members, which consists of people from all around the globe and is growing daily.

Just go to **www.MyTMMCommunity.com** and request to join The Miracle Morning Community (on Facebook). Here you'll be able to connect with others who are already practicing The Miracle Morning—many of whom have been doing it for years—to get additional support and accelerate your success. I'll be moderating the community and checking in regularly. I look forward to seeing you there!

If you'd like to connect with me personally on social media, follow **@HalElrod** on Twitter and **Facebook.com/YoPalHal** on Facebook. Please feel free to send me a direct message, leave a comment, or ask me a question. I do my best to answer every single one, so let's connect soon!

DEDICATION

This book is dedicated to all of the real estate agents and lenders who are dedicated to serving your clients to the best of your abilities, improving your abilities so that you can better serve your clients, and doing it all so that you can create the levels of personal and professional success that you truly want, and deserve.

For those of you who are committed to taking your success to the next level, we wrote this book for you.

The Miracle Morning Mission

Change One Million Lives,
One Miracle Morning At a Time

In addition to donating a percentage of the royalties earned from each copy of *The Miracle Morning for Real Estate Agents* to non-profit charities including the *Front Row Foundation* (shown below), thousands of copies of *The Miracle Morning: The Not-So-Obvious Secret Guaranteed To Transform Your Life... (Before 8AM)* are donated each year to organizations and individuals who are in need of inspiration, transformation, and guidance. Our mission is to get TMM in the hands of 1,000,000+ people so that we can literally *Change One Million Lives,*
One Miracle Morning At a Time.

Thank you so much for YOUR support!

Front RowFoundation.org

Contents

A FEW WORDS FROM
HAL ELROD

I never intended to write this book. In fact, I never intended to be an author. Growing up, if you were to have asked any of my English teachers, they would have probably voted me *least likely to finish an essay on time*, let alone pen a bestselling book! Every book I've written, including this one, is out of a sense of responsibility to pay forward the lessons that life has gifted to me.

The Miracle Morning is the one thing that has enabled me to become the person I've needed to be to achieve everything I've ever wanted for my life, and many things I once never even imagined were possible for me. And I've seen it do the same for tens of thousands of other people, particularly real estate agents. Please allow me to explain.

In 2012, the book I'd dedicated over three years of my life to writing, *The Miracle Morning: The Not-So-Obvious Secret Guaranteed To Transform Your Life… (Before 8AM)* was finally published. It quickly became not only a #1 Amazon best-seller list, but one of the highest rated books in the history of Amazon (currently with over 500 reviews, averaging 4.7 out of 5 stars). But more important was what the reviews said. People's lives were being transformed. *The Miracle Morning* was giving them the gift of being able to improve any—or literally EVERY area of their lives, and achieve new levels of success and fulfillment.

A business associate and friend of mine, Isaac Stegman, believed so strongly in *The Miracle Morning* that he generously started giving hundreds of copies to his friends in the real estate community. Surprisingly (at least it was to me), real estate agents quickly became the #1 segment of the population to start living and sharing *The Miracle Morning* amongst their peers.

In 2013 the stars align, and I connected with Honorée Corder, a huge supporter of *The Miracle Morning* and bestselling author of 13 books, including *The Successful Single Mom Book Series*. The more we talked, the more she helped me to realize that there are countless industries that may not ever hear about *The Miracle Morning*, unless I create a book series that customizes a book for each industry.

Hmm…

In 2014 the stars align yet again and this time I meet three of the world's leading real estate experts: Michael Maher, Michael Reese, and Jay Kinder. All three express an authentic passion for *The Miracle Morning* and specifically how needed it is in the real estate community. Through a series of conversations, the book that you now hold in your hands was born.

It's Your Time, This is Your Story

Know that wherever you are in your life right now is both temporary, and exactly where you are supposed to be. You have arrived at this moment to learn what you must learn, so you can become the person you need to be to create the life you truly want. Even when life is difficult or challenging—*especially* when life is difficult and challenging—the present is always an opportunity for us to learn, grow, and become better than we've ever been before.

You are in the process of writing your life story, and no good story is without a hero or heroine overcoming their fair share of challenges. In fact, the bigger the challenges, the better the story. Since there are no restrictions and no limits to where your story goes from here, what do you want the next page to say?

The good news is that you have the ability to change—or create—anything in your life, starting right now. I'm not saying you won't have to work for it, but you can quickly and easily attract and create anything you want for your life by developing into the person who is capable of doing so. That's what this book is about—helping you become the person you need to be to create everything you have every wanted for your life. There are no limits.

Grab a Pen

Before you read any further, please grab a pen or pencil so you can write in this book. As you read, mark anything that stands out which you may want to come back to later. Underline, circle, highlight, fold the corners of pages and take notes in the margins so you can come back and quickly recall the most important lessons, ideas, and strategies.

Personally, I used to struggle with this, because I am a bit of an obsessive-compulsive perfectionist and anal about keeping my things looking clean and neat. Then I realized that I needed to get over it, because the purpose of a book like this is not for it to remain untouched, but rather to maximize the value we extract from it.

Now, I mark up all of my books so I can revisit them anytime and quickly recapture all of the key benefits, without having to read the entire book again.

Okay, with your pen in hand, let's get started! The next chapter of *your life* is about to begin…

With gratitude,
Hal Elrod

AN IMPORTANT NOTE FROM MICHAEL J. MAHER

A.M. = Another Miracle.

In *(7L) The Seven Levels of Communication: Go from Relationships to Referrals*, I devote an entire chapter, *You Can't Even Spell Communicate without T, I, M, and E,* to time management. In that chapter, Rick Masters, the lead character and a real estate agent, learns about such strategies as time blocking, using your voicemail as a referral assistant, and the power of rituals - mini-habits. I describe in detail The 4 Enriching Rituals: The Sunday Night Ritual, the Nightly (Bedtime or Pre-Sleep) Ritual, the Pre-Leave (ceremoniously stopping work) Ritual and the

Morning Ritual. All of these have immense importance but the one that my coaching clients, BOOSTERS, and Ambassadors seemed to embrace the quickest was the Morning Ritual. In fact, one of our Certified Referral Coaches, Tom Cain, made the Morning Ritual one of his first lessons and action items for his clients. Download your copy of The 4 Enriching Rituals at TMMAgents.com.

Own Your Mornings; Own Your Day.

We believe that if you own your mornings, you will own your day. We encourage those we educate to focus on the start and let the momentum carry you. We were teaching a good, solid morning ritual - based on highly productive people such as Richard Branson, Tony Robbins, Oprah, and many others.

Then everything changed.

I was introduced to Hal Elrod's *The Miracle Morning*. Like Hal, I had flat-lined - literally died. I had a sheer appreciation for life and like Hal, and many others, I was broke in my 20s. These commonalities helped Hal and I hit it off from the first moment. I told him that for years "A.M." has meant Another Miracle for me and I thank God for giving me another day, another miracle, every morning. I immediately championed him to influencers in the real estate industry - Stacey Alcorn, Jack Cotton, Dave Savage, Todd Duncan, Steve Harney, Gary Keller, Steven Marshall, Pat Hiban, Tim Rhode, and others. Hal spoke for them and as expected, delivered excellent presentations.

But with his Miracle Morning, before I could teach it, I had to try it. The first week it was like somebody had given me a testosterone booster. I was on fire. Everything I touched turned to gold - every meeting was rewarding. Trust me, I was already energetic, passionate, and intense, but now I was calm while energized, controlled while passionate, and empathetic while intense. I had kept a promise to myself and the results were outstanding and every morning fills me with a sense of accomplishment.

I hope you realize this isn't about getting up earlier. It's about getting up better.

Success is simple: Find someone successful and copy their habits. The key is finding the place in your schedule to do the self-improvement habits of the highly productive and supremely successful. We know we should meditate, have quiet time, pray, do affirmations and appreciations, visualize, exercise, and journal. But who has the time?! Where do we put these things? I've taken many airplane rides over the last four years as I travel the world to spread the word of the Generosity Generation. Every single time they do the safety demonstration on the plane, the attendants say to put the oxygen mask on yourself before assisting a dependent.

This philosophy led to a blog post I titled *FLY: First Love Yourself.* If we are to first love ourselves, the only logical place to put these self-improvement practices is in the morning. Hal's *Life SAVERS* system is the answer. It's the Ultimate Morning Ritual. And in *The Miracle Morning for Real Estate Agents*, Hal got to improve his already excellent system. I got to tell the next story in Rick and Michelle's journey. And together, the authors got to not only tell you about the Miracle Morning ritual, but also, through Rick and Michelle, show you the challenges, setbacks, benefits, and successes each of you will face while adapting *your* Miracle Morning ritual.

The Miracle Morning for Real Estate Agents may make you laugh. It may make you cry. In the end, it will make you better.

Blessings,
Michael J. Maher

A HEARTFELT MESSAGE
FROM MICHAEL REESE

Gifts come in many forms in life, but not all of them are wrapped in pretty paper and have a bow on them. Some of them come in the form of challenges that require us to work at something so we can grow to become better, more well-developed versions of ourselves. Unfortunately, we often don't see the reward until we've either completed the process, or worse, completely missed out on it altogether.

The Miracle Morning for Real Estate Agents is one those types of gifts - the ones that stretch you and bless you with a better, happier, and more amazing life.

When I was given this book's predecessor, *The Miracle Morning*, the guy who gave it to me told me not to make the same mistake he did by waiting a year to read it. I'm glad he said that to me because it caused me to pick the book up and consume the pearls of wisdom on its pages way sooner than I likely would have.

It was an absolute blessing for me.

As I started to read it, I realized it contained all the elements I felt had helped me become successful in my real estate and coaching businesses. And, because I've had the unique opportunity to look into the businesses of thousands of real estate agents over the last several years, I knew this book would be a hit with them because it fundamentally deals with the number one thing you have to change in your business - yourself.

That change comes with choice, thought, and a variety of other fundamentals that need management and redirection if you're going to grow and get better. In *The Miracle Morning*, Hal laid everything out in an easy-to-read and understand format. I felt privileged to try and take the principles and make them applicable for real estate professionals.

In creating *The Miracle Morning for Real Estate Agents*, it hit me that in addition to benefiting real estate agents, the book is also going to positively impact other successful professionals in the real estate industry. They're going to want to help the people they work with by buying the book for them.

It's a tool for somebody who is in search of a better way and it will give them a step-by-step action guide to literally "download a different operating system" to run their life by. I think you'll find like I did that this is an amazing book that will change your life if you let it.

There's really not another book like this in the real estate industry. I hope you get as much enjoyment out of reading it as I did working with my co-authors to create it for you.

Michael Reese

A RESULTS ORIENTED PERSPECTIVE FROM JAY KINDER

After I read *The Miracle Morning*, the book that was the catalyst for the one you're holding in your hands, I realized that it was one of the first personal development books that gives you the "handles to the luggage" for improving the quality of your life. More specifically, it provides you with the simple, step-by-step instructions on everything you need to do to get amazing results on a consistent basis.

We all want to become better people. Obviously, you want to become a better version of yourself or you wouldn't have picked up this copy of *The Miracle Morning for Real Estate Agents*.

The tough thing about making improvements is measuring your results. If you truly want to get better, how do you know you're improving? Also, if you're shooting to get better, do you know what greatness and success look like, especially in the area of personal development? In the end, do you know how you're achieving greatness and success?

These are great questions and they're often left unanswered by the scores of books I've read in the past that aim to give you the blueprint to creating a happier, healthier, more successful version of yourself. Not only do they fail to tell you what steps you need take, in what order you need to take them, and how to take them, but they also fall short in helping you gauge your success while taking inventory of and appreciating how you've improved.

Such is not the case with *The Miracle Morning* and that's why I was excited to take the principles from that book and bring them to you in this one. In *The Miracle Morning for Real Estate Agents*, you'll get the proven process behind what you should do to get the most out of your day, live the happiest life, and have the most productivity that you could ever have in your day-to-day activities.

As a real estate agent, you have to manage and lead others every day. Your job is to add value to other people's lives and deliver leadership and results. If you can't manage yourself, then you can't do those things effectively. This book will teach you what you need to do in order to manage yourself and get the best results you can each and every day, making you the leader you were created to be.

I know you want to do these things for yourself and others; otherwise you wouldn't have purchased this book. I'm confident it will give you the roadmap you need to make it happen and to help you know, not only how to make the improvements you want in life, but also see you've achieved the results you sought.

My hope is that what's shared in this book will have as profound an impact on your life and business as it has mine.

Jay Kinder

A NOTE TO YOU

Showing is better than telling.

What you are about to immerse yourself into is a story that is loaded with actionable content. Though all characters, scenes, and scenarios are fictional and any references to real people or actual events are unintended, all lessons, results, and testimonials are based on the true accounts and experiences of top-producing real estate agents, coaching clients, and the authors. Using Maher's "Power Parable" format, like in *(7L) The Seven Levels of Communication*, we have the ability to not only tell you the strategies and tactics, like in a typical non-fiction book, but also *show* you Rick and Michelle's transformation. We hope you enjoy the story. We wrote it for you.

No matter where you are in your life and business right now, whether you're succeeding at the highest level, or if you're struggling to find your way—there is at least one thing we know that we share in common (probably a lot more than *one*, but at least one that we know for sure). We want to go to the next level. We want to improve our lives, and ourselves. This is not to suggest that there is anything *wrong* with us, but as human beings we were born with the innate desire and drive to continuously grow and improve. I believe it's within all of us. Yet, most of us wake up every day, and life pretty much stays the same.

The Miracle Morning has already shown tens of thousands of real estate agents how to transform their lives and businesses, and it can absolutely be the catalyst to transform yours. We consider it a great honor to share this with you now, and we have done everything in our power to ensure that this book will truly be a life-changing investment of your time, energy, and attention.

Thank you for allowing us to be a part of your life; a miraculous journey together is about to begin.

— 1 —
THE AWAKENING

"Get up! Let's go! Rick, I've just about had enough!"

Rick knew from the tone and volume of her voice that Michelle was serious.

He opened his eyes, rolled over, and propped himself up on the edge of the bed.

"What?!" He said groggily. He rubbed his chin full of stubble and looked up at her. Michelle was getting ready to head to her mortgage company office. She was dressed to the nines. He always loved that she could mix comfortable with classy.

But she definitely wasn't happy.

"Rick, I'm pregnant. I'm having our child in six months and I'm worried..." Michelle said softly choking back tears. "I'm worried… more about you and us than I am about the pregnancy and the baby."

Michelle NEVER cried.

He just looked up at her not knowing what to say. He stroked his unshaven chin. *What WAS wrong with him?*

Michelle wiped the single tear that had made it to the surface, regained her composure quickly, and continued, "I have to go. I have two closings today. I want you to go to this seminar. Jay Michaels from the Generosity Generation is speaking with three other fantastic speakers about something called Miracle Mornings. Lord knows, it's a miracle just to get you up in the morning! Rick, you have… or should I say, had… a good business for goodness' sakes. You know it's gone down a lot. How can you let it all go to waste?"

She put the flyer on the nightstand and was gone.

Rick contemplated rolling back into bed. He moved a half-eaten bag of chips and a book he hadn't cracked open in months aside to check the clock. *I know I set that alarm on my phone,* he thought. He must have hit snooze so many times that the alarm stopped. With a sigh, Rick grabbed the flyer, got up, and headed to the bathroom. He glanced over the flyer quickly, wadded it up, and threw it towards the trashcan five feet away. His shot missed by two feet.

"Still got it," he said sarcastically.

He heard his phone vibrate.

"God, another problem?" he said aloud. He chuckled, "Why am I talking out loud to no one? Is this the first step to insanity?" He laughed. "I just said that out loud." He laughed again as he realized he had said that out loud as well. It felt good to laugh. It had been a while. *And when was the last time Michelle laughed?*

His throat was dry and sore, most likely from snoring, so he went to the kitchen to get a drink of water. He saw a few plates from his midnight snack in the sink. While drinking the water, he noticed the clock said 8:17 a.m. He quickly attempted to figure out if he had time to go back to bed before getting ready for any appointments. He grabbed his phone and clicked on calendar to see what he had scheduled for the day. His assistant knew not to schedule anything before noon for him. As he checked to see if he had time to sleep a couple more hours, his phone started vibrating again. He looked at the number and while re-positioning his hands, accidentally hit the Talk button.

"Oh, crap," he muttered and raised the phone to his ear.

Vanessa, his assistant, was calling... again. She said, "You're going to think, 'oh crap.' I have some news for you. You might want to sit down." She said a few sentences to fill him in on what had happened.

"Oh, God!" Rick exclaimed slumping down into the dining room chair.

He ran back to the bathroom to pick up the flyer that was still wadded up on the floor.

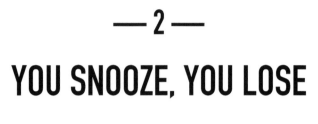

— 2 —

YOU SNOOZE, YOU LOSE

"Rick! How do you drop the ball on a million-dollar referral… FROM YOUR OWN WIFE?!" Michelle said raising her voice to him for the second time today.

After talking to Vanessa, Rick had showered and headed to Michelle's office. Now he was sitting in her office feeling like a kid in the principal's office.

"God dang it, Michelle, I don't know," Rick said, genuinely sorry. He had nobody to blame. This was on him. He was supposed to follow up with the customer and just hadn't. He was busy, but never too busy to follow up with a referral, especially a million-dollar referral. Yes, he was stressed. Yes, he was burnt out. Secretly, he knew one of the reasons was that he was going to need to wear a suit to meet this potential client and he didn't have one that fit. He'd gained 30 pounds in the last six months. *Nothing fit!*

He couldn't think of a good excuse to tell Michelle. *Ugh, I screwed up... royally.*

"Rick - to make it worse — they are considering not doing their loan with me, now. You are a reflection of me, and my business. For goodness' sakes, what are you going to do?!" Michelle said, the challenge in her voice obvious.

"Well, first of all I'm going to that seminar you suggested," Rick said.

"Yeah, right," Michelle shot back. "It starts at 8 a.m. When is the last time you were up early enough to be at something that starts at 8 a.m.?"

"I'll make it," Rick replied with false confidence.

"You'd better," Michelle said in a voice that made Rick look up at her.

The Wake-up Call

"Beep, beep, beep..." chimed Rick's smartphone. His snoring didn't miss a beat. In one fluid motion, Rick rolled over, tapped snooze, and kept sleeping.

"Rick, it's time to get up. The event is today. Get up. It's 6:30. Time to rise and shine," Michelle said, entering the room to shake him gently awake.

He rolled over and wanted nothing more in the world than for her to disappear so he could close his eyes and go back to sleep. The bed was so warm and comfortable. He was so glad he spent the extra money to get the better bed. He wiggled a little bit, closed his eyes, and started to fall asleep again when a blast of ice water hit his face and startled him awake.

"WHAT THE HELL?!" Rick yelled, water dripping down his shocked face.

"Get. Up!" Michelle, cup in hand, said firmly.

"I'm up. I'm up," Rick said wiping his face.

"Rick, you know I don't like being late," Michelle said. "I've turned the shower on for you. Let's go!"

After a shower, Rick started to feel somewhat alive. The sun started peeking through the windows. He got into his slacks, which were a little too small, put on his only button down shirt that fit, and threw on a sport jacket. The jacket fit decently but he had to wear it to cover his bulging mid-section. Even without buttoning it, he felt he pulled it off. At the very least, Michelle nodded her approval when she handed him a cup of coffee.

"We better get going," she said a few minutes later.

"We?" Rick asked.

"Yes, I'm going with you," Michelle replied. "I'm interested to see what the buzz is all about. The entire real estate community is talking about *The Miracle Morning*. Many of my clients will be there, and Don Dasick will be there. Thankfully, after you dropped the ball on those million-dollar buyers I referred to you, he was able to help me get them back as clients. Miracle of miracles!"

Rick winced at this news. Don was one of Rick's biggest rivals in the real estate world.

As they arrived at the City Convention Center, Rick reflected on how long it had been since he had been to a seminar or educational event. He knew Michelle went often and had been interviewed on stage at a couple of events recently. There were a lot of people here and Rick could feel the energy in the room.

"Rick Masters, wow. This event must be a big deal. What are you doing here?" asked Tammy Summers, a fellow Realtor.

Rick sucked his stomach in, stood up straighter, and said with confidence, "I'm just checking things out. How are you doing?"

"Fine," Tammy replied, "Looks like they are about ready to start. Michelle looks great by the way. Looks like things are well with you two."

Little does she know.

The energetic, up-tempo music playing in the room put Rick in a better mood. Between the shower, the coffee, starting to get back in the good graces with Michelle, and the music, Rick actually felt good. *How long has it been since I've had that feeling?*

Michelle walked to the very front of the room. Rick always wondered why she wanted to sit front and center. Nevertheless, he followed. He felt the eyes of the agents in the audience following him. He was known as a top producer. He had a team. From all appearances, his business and life were perfect.

Perfect…

The music stopped… Rick's heart skipped a beat…

— 3 —

TAKING LIFE HEAD ON

The music ended abruptly and a video started on the many screens throughout the large ballroom.

It started with a warning: The following video contains scenes that some viewers may find disturbing. Viewer discretion advised. Intended for mature audiences only."

Well, that certainly gets my attention...

It opened by showing a young man driving a Ford Mustang down the highway at 70 miles per hour late at night. He was dancing in his seat and had one hand in the air, conducting the music from the car's stereo. In the passenger seat slept a girl his age, presumably his girlfriend. You could feel this young man's joy as he was literally dancing in the driver's seat.

The video showed scenes from the night - the young man receiving the award for top salesperson, giving a rousing speech, and receiving a thunderous standing ovation.

The shot returned to the car and the young man bobbing his head to the music. Rick could see many of the crowd bobbing their head in rhythm with the young man on the video. Then it happened…

The scene on the video is interrupted by a Chevy truck splitting the headlights of the Mustang and hitting it head on. Rick's body jerked and he heard the entire audience groan a loud, "OH!"

The scene continued in slow motion. Airbags exploded, knocking both the driver and passenger unconscious. Rick heard gasps throughout the crowd. The Mustang spun slowly. Then, with a loud bang, a Saturn sedan driven by a 16-year old smashed into the driver side door. The crowd yelled, "OH!" again.

In slow motion, the roof of the Mustang caved into the driver's head - slicing a large V-shaped cut into the top of his head, nearly severing his left ear, and smashing his left eye socket. The Saturn smashed the door of the Mustang into the driver, breaking his arm, snapping the largest bone in his leg in half, and shattering his pelvis. The graphic video continued as many of the audience covered their eyes. Yet, they could not look away.

Blood was everywhere. The driver's body was destroyed.

Fast-forward a few minutes and the scene is loud and filled with bright lights. Emergency rescue teams are working feverishly to cut the driver's body out of the car. The body, lifeless, collapses into the arms of one of the paramedics. No breathing. No heartbeat. *Nobody could live through that!*

The body is loaded into a rescue helicopter and the paramedics get to work. The sound of the chopper rushing into the sky echoes throughout the ballroom. After a few seconds, the audience hears the heart monitor register a weak beat. The video fades to white.

The crowd sat in stunned silence. Rick saw Michelle wipe away a tear and she wasn't the only one.

The lights came on. Rick and Michelle rose to their feet with the rest of the crowd as Jay Michaels took the stage. Not cheering, but just in solemn honor.

"Wow! What an opening video, huh?!" Jay said. The crowd clapped and shook their heads.

"Please repeat after me: 'It's a great day to be alive!'" The crowd repeated it halfheartedly still recovering from the opening video.

"Let's try it again – with appreciation, with vim and vigor, and with honesty. IT'S A GREAT DAY TO BE ALIVE!"

The crowd responded loudly and with passion.

"Excellent, thank you. Please repeat after me: 'I appreciate my life!'" The crowd repeated it enthusiastically.

"Welcome to the Generosity Generation! An event that's alive and worth the drive!" Jay exclaimed. The crowd roared its approval. "Man, oh man. I love affirmations and appreciations and never have I felt them more powerfully than today after watching that video. We have a very special treat for you today. Can you believe the driver of that white Ford Mustang survived? His name is Rod Halsten. Rod was hit head-on by a drunk driver at 70 miles per hour. He broke 11 bones, suffered permanent brain damage, flat-lined for six minutes, and was told by doctors that HE WOULD NEVER WALK AGAIN. Defying the logic of doctors and the temptations to be a victim—with the love and support of his family, friends, and community—not only did Rod miraculously walk again, but he bounced back and went on to become an ultra-marathon runner — running 52 miles in one day and raising thousands of dollars for charity. I'd like all of you to give a gigantic

Generosity Generation welcome to bestselling author and my inspirational pal, Rod Halsten!"

The crowd roared. Rick even saw a few of the attendees wipe away tears as Rod took the stage.

Wow.

"Thank you so much!" Rod exclaimed and instead of the crowd sitting down, it got more enthusiastic. Rod looked at Jay and Jay just shrugged. The crowd loved it and roared again. Rick smiled. *Welcome to the Generosity Generation, Rod.*

"Truly, thank you for the warm Generosity Generation welcome! Please have a seat," Rod said again smiling. This time the crowd complied.

"Thank you, but it doesn't end there. My life didn't end that day. It does what life does. It went on…" Rod said, letting his voice trail off at the end.

He took a deep breath. "You see, even when life is difficult—in fact, especially when life is difficult—our adversity is always an opportunity for us to learn, grow, and become better than we've ever been before."

Almost as if in confession, he explained, "Recovering from my car accident wasn't the biggest challenge I've ever faced. Most people think, *but you died—what could be worse than that?* Well, it was approximately eight years later, when the United States' economy crashed, that I hit rock bottom. Now, was it just me, or did anyone else feel the effects of that?" Rod asked, sarcastically.

The crowd laughed. Rick nodded.

"Personally, it was a complete mental, financial, physical, and even spiritual breakdown. I faced financial hurdles larger than most people will ever see. I was at the lowest point in my life. You see, being complacent and settling for mediocrity had launched me into a downward spiral and deep depression. Although I knew I had to choose victory over being a victim, it was easier said than done. I had to defy mediocrity. I had to consciously accept responsibility for everything in my life so I could claim the power to change anything in my life. But, no matter how hard I tried, I just couldn't seem to turn things around."

"Then, one morning changed everything. That fateful morning, I took the advice of a friend and went on a run. I ran in an attempt to gain the clarity I needed to turn my situation around. Listen, I wasn't a runner. In fact, I despised running. That morning, I grabbed my iPod and laced up my Nike Air Jordan basketball shoes, and-," The crowd laughed. With a big smile, Rod chuckled and said, "Hey, I told you I wasn't a runner."

After more laughter, Rod pressed on, "On that run, I had one of the most powerful and profound breakthroughs of my life. Have you ever heard something time after time after time and then one day, you hear it again and it finally clicks? That's exactly what happened. On my run, I was listening to a Jim Rohn audiobook, and Jim said something that stopped me in my tracks. He said, **'Your level of success will seldom exceed your level of personal development, because success is something you attract by the person you become.'** "

Rick jolted like a bolt of electricity had hit him. Michelle grabbed his shoulder. "Are you okay?" she whispered.

"Yeah, yeah," Rick answered. "I'm fine." *What type of person had he become? By some definitions perhaps 'successful' could be used. But he had stopped developing... growing... learning.*

Rod continued, "You see, every day you and I wake up we face the same universal challenge: to overcome mediocrity and live to our full potential. It's the greatest challenge in human history—to rise above our excuses, do what's right, give our best and create the *Level 10 Life* we truly want—the one with no limits—the one that, sadly, so few people ever get to live."

Rick nodded. *I'm not living a Level 10 Life, more like a two.* He looked around and the crowd was fully engaged.

Rick heard Rod say, "Unfortunately, most people never even come close. Approximately 95% of our society settles for far less than they want in life. They wish they had more, live with regret and never really understand that they could be, do, and have all that they want.

"So, let me ask you… and I'm really asking you… are you okay with being a part of that 95%?"

"No!" came the resounding response.

Rod quickly replied, "The crucial question, then—the one that we must do whatever it takes to find the answer to—is this: *What can you start doing now to ensure that you don't end up struggling like the 95% majority will?* And are you willing to do whatever it takes to avoid a life of struggle, to join the 5% so that you can live the life you're meant to live?

"Yes!" the crowd exclaimed.

"It sounds like your unanimous answer is 'yes' and if so, let me ask you the next question, do you want to know the **three simple, yet decisive, steps** you MUST take to join those who rise above mediocrity and become the 5% who live a Level 10 Life?" Rod asked.

"YES!" Rick yelled along with the entire crowd.

"That's good because, luckily, that's the next part of my presentation," Rod quipped. The crowd laughed, again.

"**Step number one** is to acknowledge that if we don't separate ourselves from the 95%, we will end up struggling alongside them. We must embrace the fact that if we don't commit to thinking and living differently than *most people* **now**, we are setting ourselves up to endure a life of mediocrity, struggle, failure and regret—just like most people. Realize that this *will* include our own friends, family, and peers *if* we don't do something about it now and set an example of what's possible when we commit to fulfilling our potential.

"Being average means to *settle* for less than you truly want and are capable of, and to *struggle* for your entire life. Each morning, people wake up and proceed to settle for far less than they can be, and as a result, they struggle to achieve what they want. Physically, mentally, emotionally, relationally, financially - you name it - most people wake up each day and struggle to create the levels of success, happiness, love, fulfillment, health, and financial prosperity that they truly deserve. Physically, people are a mess. Obesity is at an all-time high while people look for energy in a pill, in a can, or in a cup. One out of every two marriages ends in divorce. More prescription, not to mention over-the-counter, drugs are being consumed every day in an attempt to combat depression, anxiety, and a host of other emotional and mental illnesses. Americans have more personal debt at any other time in history. Do you acknowledge that 95% of our society will never create and live the life they truly want?"

"Yes!" answered the audience.

Rod replied, "Good, then you're ready for **step number two**. Once you've been brutally honest with yourself and acknowledged that you've got to separate yourself from the 'mediocre majority,' the second step is to identify the causes of mediocrity. There are seven of them. If I were you, I'd write these down like you would write down the seven most common mistakes consumers make when choosing a Realtor!"

Rick had been taking notes and made a note to himself to also create a document for consumers titled, "The 7 Most Common Mistakes Consumers Make When Choosing a Realtor." *Thank you, Rod.*

The Seven Causes of Mediocrity

Rod kept his momentum, saying, "There are seven primary causes of mediocrity that you need to be aware of. The first is one that every person suffers from; it's called **Rearview Mirror Syndrome**. Most of us are driving through life with our subconscious mind constantly checking our own self-limiting rearview mirror, and filtering every choice we make—from what time we will wake up in the morning to which goals we will attempt—through the limitations of our past experiences. We want to create a better life, but sometimes we just don't know how to see it any other way than how it's always been. For you to fulfill your potential, it is crucial that you not only begin to see yourself as better than you've ever been before, but that you invest time daily to condition that vision of who you can become, until it truly does become your new identity.

"The second cause of mediocrity in our lives is an **Unclear Purpose**. If you ask the average person what their life's purpose is, you will usually get a funny look or a response something like, 'Gee, I don't know.' What if I asked you, right now? What would you say?" Rod asked the crowd. Rick looked at Michelle and then at the ground. *What is my purpose?*

Rod continued, "Choosing a clear purpose, one that not only inspires you to wake up every day and live your life on purpose, but that you can align all of your thoughts, words, and actions with, will be crucial in guiding you to the most successful, fulfilling life you can imagine.

"Next is something called **Isolating Incidents**. This is one of the most prevalent, yet not-so-obvious causes of mediocrity. We do this when we mistakenly assume that each choice we make, and each individual action we take, is only affecting that particular moment, or that day, but nothing could be further from the truth. We must realize that the real impact and consequence of each of our choices and actions—and even our thoughts—is monumental, because every single thought, choice, and action is determining who we are becoming, which will ultimately determine the quality of our lives.

"The fourth cause of mediocrity is **Lack of Accountability**. Consider that, as children, virtually every positive result we ever produced was thanks to the accountability provided for us by the adults in our lives. Thanks to the relentless accountability of our parents and teachers, vegetables were eaten, homework was completed, and teeth were brushed. We were bathed, and we got to bed at a reasonable hour. If it weren't for the accountability given to us, we would have most likely been malnourished, uneducated, sleep-deprived, and dirty little kids!" The crowd laughed. Rod laughed as well, and then seriously made his point, "Now that we are all grown up and striving to achieve worthy levels of success and fulfillment, we must take responsibility for initiating our own systems for accountability.

"Let me pause here and make sure you are tracking with me. Do you know someone who has perhaps let one of these bring them down? Of these first four, Rearview Mirror Syndrome, Unclear Purpose, Isolating Incidents, and Lack of Accountability, perhaps Lack of Accountability is the strongest and yet, the most easily overcome by partnering with a coach or with an accountability partner. Let's continue…"

Rick wrote down, "Get a coach or an accountability partner." *I need a coach.*

Rod continued by saying, "Next, the fifth cause of mediocrity in our lives has to do with your environment. It is having a **Mediocre Circle of Influence.** You've heard it before: we become the average of the five people with whom we spend the most time. Want to know how much money you can expect to make, how much you can expect to weigh, how happy you're going to be, or the outcome of any other area of your life? Add up the income, the weight, assess the happiness, etc. of your five closest friends, and you'll have a pretty accurate picture of what you can expect for yourself. It is crucial that we actively seek out and align ourselves with individuals who are living and performing at the level we aspire to be.

"The sixth cause, and please don't underestimate these last two as these are certainly prevalent in today's world, is **Insufficient Personal Development**. If we're measuring our success on a scale of 1-10 in any area of our lives, it's safe to say that every single one of us wants "Level 10" success. And not just in our careers, we want Level 10 health, happiness, relationships, energy — you name it. We all want to be at a Level 10 in every area. The problem is that we're trying to improve our lives without first improving ourselves. The truth is that our level of success will always parallel our level of personal development, so we must dedicate time each day to developing ourselves into a *Level 10 person*, so that we can quickly begin to attract, create, and sustain the levels of success that we truly want, and deserve.

"Lastly, the seventh and final cause of mediocrity trumps all the others. It is the number one cause of struggle, regret, and unfulfilled potential. It is the ultimate 'potential preventer' and 'destiny destroyer.' It is simply **Lack of Urgency**. It is never deciding that NOW matters more than any other time in your life. That lack of urgency prevents you from doing what's necessary today to create a better tomorrow.

"Remember this truth: now is the most important time in your life, because it's the choices you make today that are determining who you're becoming. Who you're becoming will always determine both the direction and the quality of your life. We can't continue to accept mediocrity for ourselves and put off our best until some day in the future, because that day will never come," Rod said passionately.

"Are you 100% clear on the seven causes of mediocrity and what you need to do to overcome them?" he asked the crowd.

"Yes!" the crowd exclaimed.

"So, the **first step** we take is to acknowledge and embrace the painful reality that 95% of society is struggling. If we don't commit to living and doing things differently than most people, we WILL end up struggling, like most people.

"The **second step, we just took** together when we identified the seven causes of mediocrity that you absolutely must be aware of and avoid.

"The **third step**, perhaps the most important step, will be explained before the end of the day. My time is nearing an end before the break. But let's be clear on one thing: the possibility of mediocrity exists for everyone, because being mediocre means choosing to be the same as you've always been. Mediocrity has nothing to do with how you compare to other people; it's simply a result of not making the commitment to continuously learn, grow, and improve yourself. Creating an extraordinary life begins with your commitment to learn, grow, and improve on a daily basis."

Rick shifted uncomfortably. *Holy smokes! Is he talking to me?* Out of the corner of his eye, he saw Michelle checking on his reaction to what Rod had just said. Rick tried to put on his poker face, but Michelle could always call his bluff.

Rick turned his attention back to Rod, who was continuing to speak.

"On one hand, mediocre mornings set you up for mediocre days which accumulate into mediocre weeks and months and eventually turn into mediocre years… and these mediocre mornings lead to a life of regret and unfulfilled potential. The reality is that if we don't change NOW, our life won't change. As Jay always says, 'If you want to be better off, be better.' And he's exactly right. If we don't get better, our lives won't get any better. And if we don't continuously dedicate ourselves to self-improvement, we won't get any better. Yet, most people, the 95%, wake up every day and stay the same.

"I believe you want more from your life. I know I do. No excuses…" Rod paused and said quietly, "No more excuses. No more regrets. Just an incredible, meaningful, exciting, exceptional… Level 10 Life, starting today. I can't wait to share more with you and share step three with you. Because, my friends, you deserve nothing less!"

The audience, including Rick, Michelle, and every other person in the ballroom rose to their feet and gave Rod another standing ovation.

If They Can Do It, So Can I

Jay took the stage again and shouted, "Rod Halsten everybody!" Rod took a bow and disappeared behind the stage.

"Now, I'd like to bring up to stage a few of those who have changed their lives by changing their mornings. Will Mitchell please stand up?"

Rick looked around and saw Mitchell. Mitchell was known as one of the top producers in this area.

Mitchell grabbed the microphone with confidence.[1] Rick could almost feel Mitchell's energy although they were thirty feet apart. He had never seen Mitchell on stage or speak, but Rick's impression of Mitchell was never one of confidence or energy. *More like reserved and unresponsive. What's changed in him?*

Mitchell said, "Before I started the 30-Day Challenge, I had implemented some personal growth, but I still felt like I was floating down a river with no paddle. Granted it was the right river, but I really wasn't in control. After the 30-Day Challenge, I really started to see results. It all starts from the inside. I have learned that I am in control of my destiny. My thoughts form my future. Good

---

[1] All testimonials are based on real accounts from top real estate agents. For more see Endorsements and the Bonus Chapter.

thoughts lead to good habits. Good habits lead to excellent results. Thanks to the 30-Day Challenge, I now have good habits and the results have followed. This last month, I tripled my best month in my fifteen year career as a real estate agent. I can honestly say that the 30-Day Challenge truly has been a game changer for my personal success."

Jay patted Mitchell on the back and added a disclaimer, "Remember, we can't promise you any results from anything we discuss. Most people will do nothing with what they learn and what do those 95% get from doing nothing?"

"Nothing," the crowd replied.

"Exactly," Jay acknowledged. "Next up, we have the esteemed owner of a local firm, Kazumi. You all know Kazumi as an icon in the international market. Kazumi, please come on up for a second and share your incredible story."

Kazumi looked like an owner. She took the stage like she owned it. Small in stature, she made up for any lack in height with class and posture.

Her voice was not loud but as she started to speak, you could hear a pin drop in the convention center. She spoke into the mic, "My name, in Japanese, means 'beautiful harmony,' but for a long time my life did not live up to my name. Besides being the owner of a successful brokerage, I am a mom. I have two young daughters and I also still sell homes, so I would get pulled in a million different directions throughout the day."

Rick saw Michelle lean forward and nod her head. This was hitting home for her.

Kazumi continued, "Before the 30-Day Challenge, I tended to get overwhelmed. Now, I can tell the difference on the days I do my Miracle Mornings, as I tend to stay calmer and more focused throughout the day. The difference is quite dramatic. As for the impact that the Miracle Morning 30-Day Challenge has had on growing my business; we will have 20% more agents in our organization by the end of the year since doing the 30-Day Challenge and my team will close over 50% more in sales this year than last year. I will also have personally closed over two dozen sales for my top clients, on top of running the brokerage… and being a mom.

"Thankfully, the Miracle Morning and the 30-Day Challenge enabled me to live up to my name. I feel my life is in beautiful harmony. It's so refreshing to start the day on a calm and inspiring note. Thank you."

The crowd applauded and Jay gave Kazumi a big hug.

Jay got everyone's attention, and then announced, "Our last testimonial before our break will come up in just a second, but I wanted to let you know that we have not one, but TWO very special guests speaking with you after break. I can't wait to let you know who they are and then we will have another bonus session with Rod before we wrap up the day. Can you believe we are halfway through the day already?"

"Our next top-producers are a husband-and-wife team who are rising stars in the industry. Hans and Lydia, both of you please come on up here. Hans and Lydia, everyone!"

The crowd applauded as the couple made their way to the front microphones.

Hans spoke first, "Before we discovered the Miracle Morning and the 30-Day Challenge, we never had time do all of the things we wanted to do. We could never seem to find time to work on personal development. It felt like we were just surviving each day rather than thriving. Maybe you can relate, but we often felt frustrated and unfulfilled because we wanted to get more done, but we weren't."

Lydia continued, "Our whole lives have changed since doing the 30-Day Challenge. For Hans, his business has grown from a small team to a good-sized team. He has changed offices and brokers and his team is exploding. After the 30-Day Challenge, I started a yoga class at my church. I also joined my husband's team as the Referral Specialist. I now make calls to all his past clients and run his referral business based on (7L) *The Seven Levels of Communication.* Our goals are clear, the 30-Day Challenge and Miracle Mornings have enabled us to be extraordinarily intentional about how we live every single day, and we are truly loving the life we have while creating the life of our dreams."

Lydia and Jay shared a hug on stage and the couple returned to their seats in the front row.

Jay shook his head. "I love Lydia's last sentence there. '… truly love the life we have while creating the life of our dreams…' It reminds me of something John Maxwell said. He said, 'You'll never change your life until you change something you do daily. The secret of your success is found in your daily routine.' Isn't it amazing how a simple decision, and some simple actions to change how you start each day, can change your entire life?

"Let's take our break now and do yourself a favor: talk to someone you don't know. Get to know them. Talk to those who shared their testimonials. Rod will be back up here as well. Ask him any of your questions. See you in a bit!"

SOMETHING TO THINK ABOUT

Could the Miracle Morning really be the ONE thing that can change everything? But God, why does it have to be MORNINGS?!

Michelle got up and said, "I'll grab a drink for us before the rush. We can talk about what you thought later. I saw you taking lots of notes."

Rick nodded and looked through his pages of notes. It had been a long time since he had written so much. As he went back through it, it made so much sense. *Am I a part of the 5%? Or have I fallen into the trap of the 95%?* Rick took a deep breath and stood up. He saw the crowd hovering around Rod and decided to head for the hallway snacks instead of waiting in line to talk to him.

"Whoa, Rick Masters!? What are you doing here?!"

Damion Torrento, his business partner at Rick Masters Real Estate, and Denay Clarke, his Operations Manager, both looked surprised to see him.

"Just checking things out," Rick said, noticing they both looked a bit uncomfortable. "What do you two think?"

"Um, we need to go, Rick," Damion said. "Looks like they are getting ready to start again."

Rick watched them rush off and looked into the ballroom. There was still a line to see Rod and there were people mingling throughout the halls.

"Hey, wasn't that Damion and Denay?" Michelle asked while she handed him a can of Coke.

"Yeah," Rick answered slowly.

"What did they have to say?" Michelle asked.

"Nothing," Rick said, opening his Coke. "Who's the other Coke for?"

"Me, I hope," Don Dasick said, suddenly appearing and slapping Rick on the back causing him to nearly spill the drink he just opened.

"Hello, Don," Rick said with a clinched smile.

"Looks like me and your lovely bride are going to be working together on a million-dollar deal," Don said, ignoring the cool greeting he got from Rick and grabbing the can of soda from Michelle.

"So I've heard," Rick answered, the coolness still evident in his tone.

"So, rumor has it the great Rick Masters Real Estate team is going through some changes," Don said. "Is that true?"

Rick turned to look at Michelle, but she was gone.

"Oh… you don't know yet, do you?" Don said. He laughed and said, "Where the hell have you been, Rick? Living in a cave?"

Before Rick could ask more, chimes played to signal everyone to return to their seat and Eve Sabastian, another agent in Rick's office, grabbed Don's arm and escorted him into the ballroom.

As Rick entered the room he spotted Michelle at the front with Jay. Jay put his hand on Michelle's stomach and they both laughed. Jay whispered something into Michelle's ear. Then they hugged. Did that hug last longer than normal?

— 4 —

THE AGENT WAKE UP CALL

"What did Jay say?" Rick asked Michelle as they sat down.

"What?" Michelle asked.

"What did Jay say when you were at the front just now? You know, during your *hug*." Rick asked.

Michelle stared back with a weird look on her face and whispered, "I'll tell you later."

The chimes ended and an upbeat song resounded through the ballroom. The already standing crowd clapped in unison. Jay returned to the stage. He bobbed, weaved, and conducted for a few seconds before he waved his arms and the music stopped.

"Man, what a great day!" Jay started. "And we still have more to share! Before I bring Rod back up, I want to bring up a couple of guys you ALL know. They are two of the most influential real estate agents in America and they became that way with a passion and energy combined with a never-ending love of learning. They run one of the fastest-growing real estate organizations, the National Association of Expert Advisors, and now they are here to tell you how to succeed in real estate by simply changing one small thing… Ambassadors, I want to invite you to welcome two industry icons who are here to give everyone in our profession a wake-up call, Ken Jakers and Reece Michaelson… Ken and Reece, everybody!"

"Thank you!" Reece began and the crowd stood and cheered even more. "Thank you."

"Fat, drunk, and stupid is no way to go through life, son," Ken said sharply. You could have heard a pin drop in the room.

"Who knew that a quote from Dean Warner in Animal House could start a presentation?" Ken quipped in his Texas farm boy drawl. Reece chuckled and the crowd let out a breath and chuckled with him. Ken continued, "Well, the good news is that we're not fat or stupid… 'course alcohol use is a whole 'nother conversation."

The crowd burst out laughing.

"But let's face the facts… alcoholism in the United States is 4 - 7% for normal folks, but real estate agents, oh yeah, we're a partying bunch. We come in at 9.2% for real estate agents and financial services. And I'd say we were lucky to be paired with financial services, who probably help our average. Having a drink is one thing. Being addicted to alcohol is another," Ken paused. "By a show of hands, how many of us know someone who has abused alcohol at a real estate event?"

A lot of the attendees raised their hand. *Alcohol abuse.*

Reece chimed in, "Alcohol is one thing, and divorce is another illness from which our industry suffers. Divorce rate is a full percentage point above the national average. How many of you have a friend in the business who has gotten divorced?"

Rick looked around him and nearly every hand went up. He glanced out of the corner of his eye at Michelle. She seemed to be looking straight forward. *Divorce? Are we going to become a statistic?*

Ken nodded at Reece and said, "We do a pretty good job of not being obese, but it's not our weight that kills us... it's us that kills us! Suicide for real estate agents is 1.38 times the national average. Let me repeat that y'all... 1.38 times the national average. And if we don't end it that way, we have the stress... We report high job satisfaction... 76% of us love what we do, but 73% of us reported high stress levels. The average stress level of people in the US is 4.9 on a scale of 1 to 10, but for us, we come in at 7.3. A full 20% of us rated our stress levels at 8, 9, or even 10! How many of you love what you do but experience the high levels of stress that are a big part of our profession?

Once again, most of the attendees raised their hands. *Stress.* Rick nodded his head thinking about the stresses of his job. He caught himself slouching. He felt fat. He rubbed his belly.

Reece continued, "We get some higher education, in fact our average education level is a Bachelor's Degree, but we make nearly half - half - of what the average degree-holder makes. HALF! Compared to the $1100 - $1200 per week the typical person makes after attaining a BS or BA degree, real estate agents are in the $600 per week range. How many of you know someone who used to be - used to be - in real estate - let's say in the last three years - and they are no longer in real estate because they couldn't make ends meet?"

Every hand went up in the room. *Finances.*

Ken summarized, "So we're not fat, drunk, and stupid, but we are stressed, divorced, suicidal, and broke! What if we could wave a wand and by some miracle solve all of those issues for you? Who would be interested in that type of solution?"

Rick scooted up in his chair and got his pen ready.

Agents, Are You Ready for a Wake-up Call?

Reece said, "You need to know that it's not the **best real estate agents that make the most money. It's the one with the most clients.** The mental shift you have to make is to stop working to make money, and start working for the client and working on how to find clients. It's a shift in your core belief. I believe in the strategy of pre-eminence - bringing value to people. I can just speak from personal experience. I had to change."

Rick wrote in his notes, "Focus on clients and acquiring clients."

Ken continued the thought, "The question is, **who do you have to become to hit that goal?** The agents who dedicate time to daily personal development are the agents who have the biggest success in real estate. Personal. Self. Development. The biggest, most important thing real estate agents need is clarity. Most people never find the time to do things right, and end up making the time to do things over. Learn to measure twice cut once. What things are you going to give yourself permission to not work on.[2]

Where do we allocate our resources, both human and financial? Most allocate time, energy, effort, and money in the wrong places. I didn't know success meant I had to invest in my business. The smaller costs add up… $99 for a lock box, $50 for a sign, and so on. It's a big investment to take forty listings!"

Rick nodded and he saw a lot of the audience nodding as well.

Reece picked up Ken's thought and built on it. Rick loved how they played off each other. Reece said, "From a real estate agent's perspective, having clarity and starting with productivity and time blocking is the key. Scheduling time each morning for your personal development and self-improvement is the key, so that you will become the person you need to be to create the levels of success you really want and deserve. Want Level 10 success? Start each day

---

[2] Download a free copy of The Clarity Report at www.TMMAgents.com.

by becoming a Level 10 person, and Level 10 success will begin to show up for you.

"Look at Ken's schedule! The Miracle Morning, every morning. Period. Every day. Look at my schedule. Miracle Morning, every morning. We don't just hear an idea, we implement it immediately. Once you get clarity, the next step is to take action. Remember this, it's not getting things done, it's getting the right things done, and in the right order. Take the time on the front end to get clear so you can hit your desired target. Agents, we have a wake-up call for you. Start your mornings with The Miracle Morning! Start each day by generating clarity and confidence and then GO!"

Rick, Michelle, and the entire crowd stood on their feet to celebrate the two icons.

The Third Simple, Decisive Step

Jay stepped onto the stage as the applause rippled through the ballroom. "Ladies and gentlemen, Ken Jaker and Reece Michaelson!" Jay said in his best master of ceremonies voice.

Once again, the crowd rose to its feet and applauded the two icons. Ken and Reece bounded off the stage. Rick could feel the energy in the room. Having The Miracle Morning explained in a general way was one thing, but for it to be put so explicitly and frankly by two of the real estate industry's icons was quite another. The message really hit home for him. He could tell by Michelle's reaction and the reaction of the audience that they too had awakened to the power of putting self-improvement to work in their careers, and having a time blocked off to focus on getting better as a person.

"Agents, own your morning and you'll own your day!" Jay said and pumped his fist in the air. The crowd cheered.

"Before we wrap our day, we need to have Rod re-join Ken, Reece and me on stage. Ken and Reece come on back up here. Rod, come in and give us the third, simple, yet decisive step we must take to join the 5%, escape the prison of mediocrity, live a Level 10 life, and enjoy the freedom of mastery."

Rod hopped onto the stage, gave Ken, Reece, and Jay a high-five and jumped right into his final segment. He said, "Thank you, Jay. Step three is easy. Step three is draw your line in the sand. If you don't commit to taking your life and your results to the next level now, what makes you think tomorrow, or next week, or next month will be any different? You can't wait for the perfect moment; you have to create the perfect moment. You must wake up and decide that each day is the most important day of your life, and then live it like your life depends on it… because it does."

Rick wrote down, "Draw your line in the sand. Today. Today is the most important day of my life. It's today. Can't wait for perfect moment – have to go and create it."

Rod said, "You've acknowledged and embraced the reality that 95% of society is struggling, and that if we don't commit to thinking and living differently than most people, we *will* end up struggling, like most people. You've identified the causes of mediocrity you absolutely need to remain aware of and avoid. Let me repeat, the third step is to *draw your line in the sand.* Make a decision as to what **you** are going to start doing differently from this day forward.

"Not tomorrow, not next week, or next month. You've got to make a decision **today** that you're ready and committed to making the necessary changes to guarantee that you will be able to create the life you really want. To take your personal and professional success to the level they've never been before, you have to be willing to commit at a level you've never been committed before. Are you ready to make that commitment?" Rod asked and then paused.

"Let me say that a different way… are you ready to make THAT commitment?" he repeated, with a smile.

The agents responded with a resounding, "YES!" Rick and Michelle yelling with the rest.

"Your entire life changes the day that you decide you will no longer accept mediocrity for yourself. When you realize that today is the most important day of your life. When you decide that now matters more than any other time. Because it is who you are becoming each day based on the decisions that you are making and the actions that you are taking, that is determining who you are going to be for the rest of your life."

I don't want to be the same as I've been lately. Michelle and I can't be the same as we always have been. It's time to end this slump.

Rod walked over until he stood right in front of Rick and Michelle. He said, "We've all experienced the pain of regret—as a result of thinking and talking ourselves into being, doing, and having less than our true potential. As I said before, mediocre months inevitably turn into mediocre years, and if we don't change who we are now, our self-created fate will be a life of mediocrity and unfulfilled potential, accepting less from ourselves, and for our lives, than we truly want… and deserve.

"The reality is that if we don't change **now,** our life won't change. If we don't get better, our life won't get better. If we don't consistently invest time into our self-improvement, our life will not improve. Yet, most of us wake up every day and stay the same," Rod said. *I can literally feel his passion.*

Rod paused to gather himself and then said, "I think you want more for your life. I know I do. If you're being completely honest with yourself, you truly want to live an extraordinary life. That doesn't necessarily mean being rich or famous. Everyone's dream is different. What it does mean is living your definition of an extraordinary life. A life where you get to call the shots, and live life on your terms, with the freedom to do, be, and have *everything* you've ever wanted for your life. No excuses. No regrets. Just an incredible, meaningful, and exciting life! FREEDOM! Do you want freedom?!"

"YES!" yelled the crowd. Rick and Michelle yelled as well. *Could it be as easy as getting started right and having a morning ritual? I know I've heard that before but never so… completely. Could controlling my morning help me control my life?*

"Yes," Rod continued. "We all do. As stated so truthfully by bestselling author, Robin Sharma: **'One of the saddest things in life is to get to the end and look back in regret, knowing that you could have been, done, and had so much more.'** While this is the self-imposed fate of the masses, it absolutely does not have to be yours. Today you can draw your line in the sand. You can decide that mediocrity is no longer acceptable for **you.** You can claim your greatness. You can choose to become the person you need to be, to create the extraordinary life that you truly want. Your life can be filled with an abundance of energy, love, health, happiness, success, prosperity, and everything else that you've ever imagined having, doing, or being. *The Miracle Morning 30-Day Challenge* can give you that life…."

"It did for me," chimed Reece.

"It did for me," said Ken.

"It did for me," Jay repeated. "Let's hear from a few others[3] who also put their lives into hyper-drive by taking control of their self-improvement and their mornings."

Daphne, a top-producing Realtor, stepped onto stage and was handed the mic.

"I've been waking up and implementing the Miracle Morning for about six weeks and my life is forever changed. Every morning I am energized, and ready to take on the day with a positive mindset.

---

[3]   All testimonials are based on real accounts from top real estate agents. For more see Endorsements and the Bonus Chapter.

I have practiced the Miracle Morning activities followed by the 1st & 10 as described in *(7L) The Seven Levels of Communication: Go from Relationships to Referral*[4] and… WOW! My life is on fire! I've lost one-half of a dress size. I'm eating healthier. I've read two books. I've reconnected with my people and my team's production is skyrocketing! In the past ten days we have had nine contracts accepted on behalf of both buyers and sellers, and in some cases both, seller sold home and purchased another! My affirmations are becoming reality and the life that I visualize is coming to fruition. I am grateful for these leaders. Thank you all!"

Rod bowed and Jay nodded. Reece and Ken said, "Thank you!"

Jay brought up the next top agent by announcing, "Steve does over 200 transactions per year and is one of the top agents in the country. He's here to share his 30-Day Challenge story."

Steve followed Daphne onto the stage and took the microphone, "Before Miracle Morning, I woke up in the morning early to prospect. However, I had no real plan. Everything was sporadic and chaotic. Now, with Miracle Morning and having taken the 30-Day Challenge, I have a plan and a system to be more productive in my business, and more importantly in life. So far, I have lost 22 pounds and I'm on my way to losing 50. I get up every morning and workout as part of my Miracle Morning. I am more organized and am helping more people. I tell everyone I know about the 30-Day Challenge and have referred over 60 people so far. I truly believe that the Miracle Morning 30-Day Challenge is a way to change your destiny."

"Thank you Steve!" Jay introduced the next top producer, by saying, "Esmeralda is one of the top agents in the world with expansion teams across the globe and she's here to share her Miracle Morning story."

---

4 The 1st & 10 is the habit of calling ten people first thing in the morning, rather than checking email, opening the computer, or having meetings. More strategies at www.MiracleMorningAgent.com

Rick could tell she had stage experience. She was comfortable and immediately likeable. "Ever since I completed the Miracle Morning 30-Day Challenge, I'm healthier, less stressed, focused, and finally have clarity in my life. I hated running but I decided to sign up for a 5K race, and then it became a game. Now, I've done two 5Ks in the last two months! Yea me!" She threw her hands into the air and laughed. The audience loved it and laughed with her.

"As far as business, I'm so much more energetic, so I get more done. I'm less stressed. I love the clarity I get when I'm doing my morning ritual - especially during running. We continue to open new teams around the globe and that requires energy, focus, and clarity. The Miracle Morning 30-Day Challenge gives me all of that. I had my entire inside sales team do the 30-Day Challenge and there was a huge difference in their productivity - and happiness. Here's the last thing I'd like to say: Give it 30 days and see what happens. There are a million reasons to do it. Remember, 90-95% of CEOs get up before 6 a.m. and high achievers have a morning ritual. Make it happen. Thanks for having me!"

Jay nodded to the three top agents who had shared their stories. He joined the crowd in giving them a resounding round of applause.

"Now is your chance. You've heard from many of the biggest producers in the real estate industry and you've seen the man himself, Rod Halsten. The best investment you can make is an investment in yourself. It's an investment that pays you over and over again. There is no better place to invest than into your self-improvement and into your mornings. The Generosity Generation volunteers are set up just outside to help you get started with the 30-Day Challenge. Now is the time to rise and shine agents! Rise... and... shine!

Jay gave Ken, Reece, and Rod a high-five, and passionately started his closing, "Have a great day agents! Rise, get up, get going and shine, use your talents and perform at your highest level -

at Level 10! We hope you take us up on this opportunity to live a life of no regrets of having a place and a plan for YOUR self-improvement and your personal development so YOU can be all you can be, do all you want to do and have all you want to have! Rise and shine!"

Rick followed the rush out into the hall and luckily stepped right out to one of the tables. He didn't even hesitate. THIS was the answer.

"Hey!" Michelle said as she came up behind him as he was signing.

"Hey!" Rick said with more energy than he'd felt in a while.

"Great that you signed up," Michelle said. Rick could tell she was impressed he took the initiative to sign up without talking to her first. Normally with such a large purchase, he'd discuss it, but he knew she would support his 30-Day Challenge wholeheartedly.

Little did he know *how* wholeheartedly she would support him.

MIRACLE MORNING (DAY 1): THE SOUND OF SILENCE

"What the heck?!!" Rick shouted. He and Michelle sat up in their bed at the sound of the fire alarm blaring throughout the house. Rick got up and did a complete tour of the house. Nothing was on fire or smoking. He finally got the alarms silent after taking out a couple of batteries. By then, it was 30 minutes before their first call.

"You going back to bed?" Rick asked Michelle.

"No," Michelle answered and went to the kitchen to start the coffee.

"Why not?" Rick asked. "You need your rest."

"I signed up for the 30-Day Challenge too!" Michelle hollered from the kitchen.

"What? You're not an agent. Why?" Rick said as he joined her in the kitchen.

"I wanted to," Michelle answered wearily. "This isn't just for real estate agents, Rick. It's about maximizing mornings and whether I'm an agent, a mortgage professional, or anyone else, I now see how crucial mornings are for me - and us. Also with the baby coming, I wanted to be as prepared as possible. Maybe I can keep doing what I'm doing even with having a baby."

Rick felt horrible. He knew that Michelle was doing this - trying to do more - because she was worried about him and his business. He wasn't keeping up his end of the deal in their marriage and he knew it. He also knew she would be his toughest accountability partner. No faking like he was up for calls. He was going to have to get up and show up! *Here we go… it's time to rise and shine.*

The First Call of the First Morning of the First Day of the Rest of Your Life

Their Miracle Morning Coach greeted everyone with a cheerful, "Good Miracle Morning everyone! Time to rise and shine!"

"Good morning!" responded many on the call. *Why so dang cheerful?* Rick looked at Michelle and shrugged. Michelle winked and smiled. *She seems to be enjoying this.*

"Why did you get up this morning?" Coach asked. Rick waited for him to continue but it was like he was waiting for the answer. *Why did I get up this morning?*

"Fire alarm," Rick heard himself say. Michelle chuckled.

"What was that?" Coach said through the answers.

"We woke up because the fire alarm was blaring," Rick said. Michelle laughed again.

"Well, that's a first," Coach said. "Hope everything is okay there."

"All good," Rick said.

"We all need a fire alarm in our life every once in a while, don't we?" Coach said. Rick and Michelle had to nod.

"Why did you bother getting out of bed this morning? Think about that for a second... Why do you wake up most mornings? Why do you leave the comfort of your warm, cozy bed? Is it because you *want to*? Or do you delay waking up—until you absolutely *have to*?"

Coach said, "If Rick and Michelle hadn't heard the fire alarm, would they have just gotten up on their own and attended this call and attacked their day? If you're like most people, you wake up to the incessant beeping of an alarm clock or smartphone each morning and reluctantly drag yourself out of bed because you *have to* be somewhere, do something, answer to—or take care of—someone else. Given the choice most people would continue sleeping." Rick looked at Michelle and winked. Michelle did not wink back.

You Snooze, You Lose: The Truth about Waking Up

Coach continued, "So naturally, we rebel. We hit the snooze button and resist waking up, unaware that our resistance is sending a message to the universe that we'd rather lie there in our beds, unconscious, then consciously and actively live and create the lives we claim that we want."

"The old saying, 'you snooze, you lose' may have a much deeper meaning than any of us realized. When you delay waking up until you *have* to—meaning you wait until the last possible moment to get out of bed and start your day—consider that what you're actually doing is **resisting your life**. Every time you hit the snooze button, you're in a state of resistance to your day, to your life, and to waking up and creating the life you say you want. It's as if you're saying, 'I don't want to live my life, at least not to the fullest.' Now, I know you may have never thought of it that way, but that's not the message you want to send, is it?" Coach asked. He waited for an answer again.

A resounding, "No!" came from the listeners.

Coach took a second and then continued, "The tone of our morning has a powerful impact on the tone of the rest of our day. It can become a cycle: waking up with despair, spending the day continuing to feel that way, going to sleep feeling anxious or depressed, then repeating the cycle of melancholy the next day. Ugh!

"On the other hand, when you wake up each day with passion and purpose, you join the small percentage of high achievers who are pursuing and living their dreams. **Most importantly, you will wake up happy, energized, and on purpose**. But don't take my word for it—trust these famous early risers: Oprah Winfrey, Tony Robbins, Bill Gates, Howard Schultz, Deepak Chopra, Wayne Dyer, Thomas Jefferson, Benjamin Franklin, Albert Einstein, Aristotle, and many others. That includes top producers in your industry, some of whom you heard at the Generosity Generation event.

"No one in the real estate business ever taught us that by learning how to consciously set our intention to wake up each morning with a genuine desire—even enthusiasm—to do so, we can change not only our careers, but our entire lives.

"When are you going to develop yourself into the person you need to be to create the levels of health, wealth, happiness, success, and freedom that you truly want and deserve? When are you going to actually live your life instead of numbly going through the motions looking for every possible distraction to escape reality? What if your reality—your life—could finally be something that you can't wait to be conscious for?" Coach asked with passion. He paused.

"Take a moment now to write down the moments in your life when you have woken up thrilled, excited, and ready to go," Coach assigned.

Michelle started writing. Rick couldn't wait to read what she wrote. He looked down at his blank sheet. He couldn't remember the last time he woke up thrilled, much less even remotely excited about his life.

"Coach?' said a voice on the call.

"Yes?" replied Coach.

"This is Marianne from Stamford, Connecticut."

"Go ahead, Marianne!" Coach said.

"I just have to say that this morning had me excited. I was so nervous about waking up on time, I woke up on my own an hour before my alarm went off," Marianne said excitedly. "This might sound silly, but waiting for this call and this program to start felt like when I was a kid on Christmas morning! I so need this!"

Dozens of people on the call agreed. Resounding, positive comments echoed on the line. Rick rolled his eyes. Michelle caught Rick mid-eye roll and frowned in disapproval. *Geez.*

The Secret to Making Every Morning Feel Like Christmas

Clearly picking up on the energy of the group, Coach forged ahead: "Think back to a time in your life when you were genuinely excited to wake up in the morning. Maybe it was to catch an early flight for a vacation that you had been anticipating for months. Maybe it was your first day at a new job, or your first day of school.

Maybe it was your wedding day, or your last birthday. Maybe it was to play softball or get in a round of golf. Personally, I can't think of any time in my life when I was more excited to wake up in the morning—regardless of how much sleep I got—than when I was a kid, every year on Christmas morning. Maybe you can relate?" Coach reminisced. Rick nodded. *Was I excited last Christmas?*

"It doesn't matter what the situation was that brought about your excitement, the important thing is to think - how did you feel when those mornings arrived? Did you have to drag yourself out of bed? Doubtful. On mornings like these, we can't wait to wake up! We do so feeling energized and genuinely excited. We quickly throw the covers off and spring to our feet, ready to take on the day! Imagine if this is what *every day* of your life was like. Shouldn't it be? It can. We can attack every day with energy and excitement. The first step to getting up feeling energized is setting yourself up for success the previous night."

How to Wake Up With More Energy (On Less Sleep)

Coach continued, "In your 30-Day Challenge Fast-Start Kit, you received the Pre-Sleep Affirmation. How many of you read this last night?"

Rick looked at Michelle. They didn't receive the 30-Day Challenge Fast-Start Kit.

Amid the "yeses," there were a few who, like Rick and Michelle, hadn't received their kit. Coach gave everyone a phone number to call to get the kit, reminded them that these could be downloaded from TMMAgents.com and then asked everyone who had their kit to turn to the page titled **Bedtime Affirmations**. [Note: For a printable edition of the Bedtime Affirmations, please go to www. TMMAgents.com.]

He asked for a volunteer to read the affirmation for those who didn't get kits. Dave, an agent from Indiana, responded first.

He read:

"Read these powerful affirmations <u>every</u> night before bed, and you will FEEL the difference when you wake up!

"FIRST: I have completed all of my daily tasks to prepare myself for tomorrow, including setting everything out that I need for my Miracle Morning. My alarm clock is across the room so I will have to get out of bed to turn it off, I have decided what time I am waking up, and have clarity as to specifically what I will do when I wake up. I am anticipating the morning with positive expectations and excitement, because I am well aware of the benefits that I will receive by choosing to wake up and live The Miracle Morning. The Miracle Morning is allowing me to become the person I need to be to easily and consistently attract, create, and sustain the life that I truly want.

SECOND: I am going to bed tonight at __:___ PM and waking up at __:___ AM, which gives me __ hours of sleep. This is PLENTY; in fact, it is exactly what I need in order to perform at a peak level tomorrow. The reality is, my mind controls my body, and I really only need as much sleep as I tell myself that I need. Many of the most successful people in history have functioned optimally on 4-6 hours of sleep, and I cannot allow myself to fall into the limiting belief that sleeping *more* will somehow improve my life. In fact, it will be seriously detrimental to my stress level, finances, relationships, career, and lifestyle goals. My quality of life as I know it depends on my waking up on time tomorrow.

THIRD: I am waking up tomorrow morning at __:___ AM because by doing so, I significantly increase the likelihood that I will achieve my goals this week, this month, this year, and for the rest of my life. I am committed to waking up on time tomorrow because #1: Doing so will enable me to develop the discipline I need to succeed in all areas, and #2: I know that how I start each day determines how I create my life, because my day *is* my life. I can no longer accept anything less than my best from myself.

FOURTH: Regardless of how long it takes to fall asleep, what I dream about, how tired or overwhelmed I feel right now, or when I wake up, I will energetically spring out of bed tomorrow morning at __:___ to create the most extraordinary life I can imagine—the life I deserve to live."

Coach chimed in, "Thank you Dave. Agents, use the Bedtime Affirmations to prepare your mind for waking up early and feeling energized. Now, I am going to cover how to actually make sure you get out of bed. This is for you Snooze-aholics!" Coach said.

Rick and Michelle laughed. Rick pretended to be upset, mouthing "What?" to Michelle. *Hi, I'm Rick, and I'm a Snooze-aholic.*

"It's been said that very few people actually likes waking up early, but everyone loves the feeling of having gotten up early. Kind of like exercising—many of us struggle to get ourselves to the gym, but all of us love the feeling of having gotten in a good workout. Waking up early, especially when done with a commitment to self-improvement, always starts you off feeling empowered for your day.

"For most of us, when the alarm clock or smartphone alarm sounds each morning, we are awakened from a dead sleep. Leaving the comfort of our beds is the least appealing thing to do. The challenge is, how do you give yourself the motivation you need to wake up early and create an extraordinary day?

"The answer is simple: one step at a time. What I'm going to give you now is what I call **The Five-Step 'Snooze-Proof' Wake Up Strategy**. These are five simple steps, so easy to do that they will make waking up in the morning—even *early* in the morning—easier than it's ever been for you.

Step 1: Set your intentions before you go to bed.

Remember that a Miracle Morning always starts the night before, with your commitment to waking up on time and the intentions you set as far as how you will feel when you wake up. The first key to waking up energized and ready to take on your day is to remember this: *Your first thought in the morning is almost always the last thought you had before you went to bed.* We've covered this with the Bedtime Affirmation.

Step 2: Move your alarm across the room.

As simple as it may be, this one really is a game changer. Ideally, place it in or on the way to your bathroom. I don't care who you are—myself included—if you keep your alarm clock or your smart phone next to your bed, then you're going to be half asleep when it goes off. And half asleep is not the state you want to be in when you are making that crucial decision whether to wake up and maximize your morning, or keep sleeping and waste it. This forces you to get out of bed and engage your body in movement. Movement creates energy, so when you get up and walk across the room to turn off your alarm clock, it naturally helps you to wake up and keep moving forward.

Step 3: Brush your teeth.

I know what you're thinking. Wow, glad I signed up to be told to BRUSH MY TEETH! In all seriousness, don't let the fact that this might sound like I'm parenting get in the way of you doing it." Rick and Michelle laughed out loud and realized they weren't on mute.

"Sorry," Rick said, putting the phone on mute. Rick and Michelle looked at each other like little kids who had just got caught with their hand in the cookie jar.

Coach responded, "To some, this may seem funny. You've been told to brush your teeth all your life as a way to avoid cavities, but never as a way to wake up. To recap, as soon as you've gotten out of bed to turn off your alarm, go directly to the bathroom sink to brush your teeth. While you're at it, splash some water on your face. And if you really want to accelerate your wake up, swish some mouthwash around in your mouth! The point is not that these are advanced steps—in fact, they are quite the opposite. The point is that you have a handful of steps that are so easy to do, they will soon become programmed into your subconscious. Even on days when you wake up feeling tired, you can easily, almost *mindlessly* move through them. Before you know it, you're feeling awake and ready to take on your day.

Step 4: Drink a full glass of water.

This is one of the most important steps, and you should do it as soon as possible after waking. After six to eight hours without water, you'll naturally be a little dehydrated, and dehydration causes fatigue. So, it's crucial that you hydrate yourself first thing every morning. Start by getting a glass of water and then chug it! Drink it as fast as is comfortable for you. The objective is to rehydrate your body and mind as fast as possible, to replace the water you were deprived of during the hours you slept. The documentation and research about the benefits of drinking a large glass of water in the morning is overwhelming.

"Can't you just imagine starting every morning with getting out of bed, walking across the room to turn off the alarm, making your way to the sink to brush your teeth, and then drinking the large cup of water that was sitting next to the sink?"

Coach let that vision set in with the listeners and then taught the final step. He said, "You're probably good to go, but if not, complete this last step, which actually has two options from you to choose from.

Step 5: Get dressed in your workout clothes.

Most get dressed, and some even sleep in their workout clothes. Some need a more startling and shocking approach so they jump into the shower. A lot of people prefer the morning shower because it helps wake them up and gives them a 'fresh' start to the day. I am a firm believer that you should *earn your morning shower* by breaking a sweat, but you can do whatever works for you.

"Please note this in your Miracle Morning Journal: Start tonight by reading the Bedtime Affirmation, moving your alarm clock or phone across the room, setting your toothbrush and toothpaste out, placing a large cup of water on your sink, and either having your workout clothes out or your towel for the shower ready."

"These five steps are simple, easy to do, and they can be the difference maker in your ability to develop the habit of waking up early and on time, every morning."

Rick had to admit he felt better having the steps in place to get a good start to the morning, but wondered what he was supposed to do after changing into his workout clothes.

The Life S.A.V.E.R.S.

"There are six practices that make up The Miracle Morning, organized into a memorable acronym: S-A-V-E-R-S. While these practices make up the fundamental structure of The Miracle Morning, I'm going to go beyond the original Miracle Morning/ SAVERS concepts, over the course of our training. I'm going to give you advanced strategies that will help you to take your Miracle Morning to levels that most Miracle Morning practitioners have not yet been taught how to do. For example, on our next call I'll teach you a brand new formula that Rod just developed for increasing the effectiveness of your affirmations.

"But for today, let's start with the first 'S' in SAVERS," Coach said, his voice trailing off.

S is for...

"I know what you might be thinking, but no - the first 'S' is not for *snooze*, nor is it for *sleep*. Sorry! While I know many people would love it if they could sleep their way to success, unless you have been cryogenically frozen and are awaiting a large inheritance at the time of being thawed out—life just doesn't work that way."

Rick and Michelle looked at each other and smiled. Then, the line got quiet. Coach stopped talking. A few seconds passed, which felt like a lot more. Then, suddenly…

"SILENCE!" Coach pierced the silence with one word. Rick and Michelle were both startled from writing in their journals.

"Silence is the first practice of the Miracle Morning. Silence is the first of the six *Life SAVERS*," Coach said. Rick wrote, "Silence" in his journal. *Start with Silence? I think I liked the idea of more sleep!*

"Mahatma Gandhi once said, 'In the attitude of silence the soul finds the path in a clearer light, and what is elusive and deceptive resolves itself into crystal clearness.' And author Matthew Kelly said, 'You can learn more in an hour of silence than you can in a year of books' which is quite a profound statement if you think about it. Consider the wisdom in a year's worth of books! Can silence and meditation be even more powerful?

"Silence may be one of the most significant areas for improvement in our noisy, fast-paced businesses and over-stimulated lifestyles. I'm referring to the life-transforming power of purposeful Silence. *Purposeful* simply means that you are engaging in a period of Silence with a highly beneficial purpose in mind— not just for the heck of it.

"As Reece and Ken mentioned at the Generosity Generation event, real estate agents rate their jobs and lives as extremely stressful. If you want to immediately reduce your stress levels, begin each day with the kind of calm, clarity, and peace of mind that will allow you to stay focused on what's most important in your life. You need to do the opposite of what most people do and instead of just getting up and jumping into chaos, start every morning with a period of purposeful Silence.

"The life-enhancing benefits of Silence have been well documented throughout the ages. From the power of prayer, to the magic of meditation, some of the greatest minds in history have used purposeful Silence to transcend their limitations and create extraordinary results. In fact, some of the most successful people in the world swear by Silence and meditation.

"Russell Simmons, the co-founder of Def Jam Records—who, by the way, has an estimated net worth of $340 million—wrote the bestselling book, *Success Through Stillness*. In the opening pages, he wrote, 'I consider meditation to be the most effective tool you can employ to build success in your life.'

"Ellen DeGeneres said that she meditates every day, because it makes her feel good. Billionaire, Ray Dialio, founder of the world's largest hedge fund firm, said, 'Meditation, more than anything in my life, was the biggest ingredient of whatever success I've had.'

"Pretty profound statements, right?! When you hear this, it makes you consider that the most untapped technique for taking your success to the next level, just might be starting your day with a little Silence."

How Do Your Mornings Usually Begin?

Coach took a drink of water and continued, "Do you invest time in centering yourself and creating an optimum state of mind to lead you through the rest of the day? Or do you usually wait to wake up until you've got something to do? Do the words calm, peaceful, or rejuvenating describe your average morning? If they do, congratulations! You're already a step ahead of the rest of us."

Rick and Michelle looked at each other. Knowing the line was on mute, Rick asked, "How do you start your mornings?" He didn't know because Michelle got up much earlier than he did.

Michelle answered, "I wouldn't call it 'Purposeful Silence,' but I like the quiet of the mornings. I sit and drink coffee in my robe.

No television. No radio. Just the sounds of nature or absolutely quiet. Even before I eat, I take some time to just be still. I really enjoy my mornings."

Rick nodded, almost surprised at how much more together Michelle seemed to have her life than he did. Sure, they slept in the same bed, ate meals together, were married to each other, but yet somehow he wasn't on the same level as her. He had fallen behind.

Coach was still instructing. He said, "For most of us, words like rushed, hectic, stressful or even chaotic might best describe our typical mornings. For others, slow, lazy, and lethargic might be a more accurate description of how the morning begins. Which of these scenarios best describes your average morning? Write down one or two words that describe your mornings."

Without hesitation, Rick wrote down "Mediocre." As usual, Michelle was a bit more thoughtful, and after a few moments of consideration, she wrote down "Peaceful."

After a minute, Coach continued, "Silence is one of the best ways to immediately reduce stress, while increasing your self-awareness and gaining the clarity that will allow you to maintain your focus on your goals, priorities, and what's most important for your life, each and every day.

"Here are some activities to choose from and practice during your period of Silence: Meditation… Prayer… Reflection… Deep Breathing… and my favorite—Appreciation. All of these practices will relax your mind and body, calm your spirit, and allow you to be totally present and open to receiving the benefits from the remaining *Life SAVERS,* which make up the rest of your Miracle Morning.

"Let me go into a little more depth on one of these: the essence of meditation is simply silencing or focusing the mind for a period of time. You may or may not be aware of all the extraordinary health benefits of meditating. Study after study shows that, in many cases, meditation can be more effective than medication. Studies link regular meditation to improving metabolism, lowering blood pressure, increasing brain activation, and other significant improvements for your mental and physical well-being. It can alleviate stress and pain, promote sleep, enhance focus and concentration, and even increase your lifespan."

Coach's Wisdom

"Consider that when we reach the end of our lives, we won't wish we'd spent more time at the office, had more money, or bought more 'things.' As we grow older, we become more aware of how distracted we've been, focusing on the pursuit of things that we think will make us happy, while missing the truth that *we already have everything we could ever need to be the happiest we could ever be.* It's simply up to us to remember that truth in each moment. We must realize that our happiness doesn't come from building wealth or collecting things, but from being present to all that we have, all that we are, and all that we can become. Daily meditation is the gateway to connect with your highest self, realize your deepest truth, and ultimately to start experiencing all that life has to offer… NOW.

"Meditation also requires very little time. You can take advantage of the benefits of meditation in just a few minutes a day," Coach said.

"And while you don't have to choose meditation during your period of Silence, enough people do that we have a simple, step-by-step plan for you," Coach said, referencing a page in the Kit. "Dave, would you mind reading this for those who don't have the kit yet? Also, everybody remember that if you haven't done so yet, be sure to go to **www.TMMAgents.com** to download your 30-Day Challenge Fast-Start Kit.

Dave read the page:

Miracle Morning Meditation

"Here is a simple, step-by-step individual meditation that you can use during your Miracle Morning, even if you've never meditated before:

Prepare:

Before beginning your meditation, it's important to prepare your mindset and set your expectations. This is a time for you to quiet your mind and let go of the compulsive need to constantly be thinking about something—either reliving the past, stressing or worrying about the future—but never living fully in the present. This is the time to let go of your stresses, take a break from worrying about your problems, and be fully present in this moment. It is a time to access the essence of who you truly are—to go deeper than what you have, what you do, or the labels you've accepted as 'who you are'—which most people have never even attempted to do. Accessing this essence of who you truly are is often referred to as 'just being.' Not thinking, not doing… just being. If this sounds foreign to you, or too 'new-age' that's okay. I used to feel the same way. It's probably just because you've never tried it before. But thankfully, you're about to.

Sit:

Find a quiet, comfortable place to sit. You can sit up straight on a chair, cross-legged on the floor, or sit on a pillow, for added comfort. Don't worry too much about how you sit, just make sure that your spine is as straight as possible. Resist any temptation to slump, slouch, or lean. You can close your eyes, or you can look down at the ground, approximately two feet in front of you.

Focus on Your Breath:

Begin by focusing on your breath, taking slow, deep breaths. In through the nose, out through the mouth, and be sure to breathe into your belly, rather than your chest. The most effective breathing should cause your belly to expand, and not your chest.

The 3-3-3 Breathing Technique:

Now, start pacing your breath; in slowly on a count of three seconds (one, one-thousand, two, one-thousand, three, one-thousand)... hold it in for three seconds (one, one-thousand, two, one-thousand, three, one-thousand)... and then breathe out slowly on a count of three seconds (one, one-thousand, two, one-thousand, three, one-thousand). Feel your thoughts and emotions settling down as you focus on your breath. Be aware that as you attempt to quiet your mind, thoughts will still come in to pay a visit. Simply acknowledge them, then let them go, always returning your focus to your breath.

Allow Your Thoughts to Be as They Are:

Remember, this is a time for you to let go of your compulsive need to constantly be thinking about something. This is a time to let go of your stress and take a break from worrying about your problems. This is the time to be fully present in this moment. This is often referred to as just being. Not thinking, not doing... just being. Continue to follow your breaths, and imagine inhaling positive, loving, peaceful energy, and exhaling all of your worries and stress. Enjoy the quiet. Enjoy the moment. Just breathe... Just be.

If you find that you have a constant influx of thoughts, it may be helpful for you to focus on a single word or a phrase, and repeat it over and over again to yourself, as you inhale and exhale. For example, you might try something like: (On the inhale) 'I breathe in peace...' (As you exhale) 'I breathe out love... I breathe in peace...' (Inhale)... 'I breathe out love...' (Exhale)... You can swap the words peace and love with whatever you feel like you need bring more of into your life (confidence, faith, energy, belief, etc.), and whatever you feel like you want to give more of to the world."

Coach gave a few minutes for everyone to take notes, then continued, "Thank you again, Dave. Agents, meditation is a gift you can give yourself every day and it truly is an incredible one. My time spent meditating has become one of my favorite parts of my day. It is a time to be at peace, to experience gratitude and appreciation, and a time of freedom from our day-to-day stressors and worries. Think of daily meditation as a temporary vacation from your problems. While your problems will still be there when you finish your daily meditation, you'll find that you are much more centered and better equipped to solve them.

"Take a moment now to take a few deep breaths in through your nose and out your mouth. Breathe in for a count of two and breathe out for a count of four," Coach instructed.

Rick and Michelle both inhaled deeply through their nose and then slowly let it out through their mouth. Rick felt himself sitting up straighter and feeling less stressful after just a couple of deep breaths. *Amazing.*

Coach interrupted everyone's breathing practice to conclude their work on Silence. He softly said, "There's no single right way to spend time in Silence. You can pray, meditate, focus on what you're grateful for, or even engage in deep thought. However, I want to warn you. Silence is a practice and as a practice, you may struggle with this in the beginning. You might sit in Silence, but your mind won't stop racing. You will get better with practice. Don't be discouraged if spending time in Silence, or meditating, is at first a challenge for you. This is why we cover it first. You will start with 5 minutes of Silence and then you can adapt your practice to as little as 60 seconds to as much as 60 minutes! By the end of your 30-Day Challenge, you will be able to go 'to a more peaceful place' at any time you want, perhaps before an appointment with a client or during negotiations. You will realize a life of more peace, clarity, and focus.

You can also revisit your meditation practice throughout the day.

When you feel stressed or need to reset your mind, take a minute to pay attention to your breath, and return your mind to the present moment. Try taking a walk, and instead of thinking about things you need to do later, pay attention to your breath, your body's sensations, the things around you. When you eat, just eat, and focus your attention on the food, on your feelings as you eat, on the sensations. Wash your dishes and sweep your floor mindfully.

Most importantly, be present with your loved ones.

Make every person you're with feel like they are the most important person in the world. Many Realtors who have been through the 30-Day Challenge now use their meditation before listing appointments, buyer consultations, and their Hour of Power calls. We are going to cover all six practices of S.A.V.E.R.S. in future calls but I want your focus to be Silence right now. Get in tune with just being... Now, so that you get used to the rhythm of the six practices put together, I want to briefly cover the 6-Minute Miracle Routine.[5]"

Rick could hear Coach take a deep breath. Coach then led them through the 6-Minute Miracle Routine, a short, but powerful sequence of Silence, Affirmations, Visualization, Exercise, Reading, and Scribing. Rick had never felt so calm, yet motivated in his entire life. He could tell Michelle was feeling the same way. *This is good.*

"That's our call for today, ladies and gentlemen. Focus on your Silence during your Miracle Morning tomorrow. Rise and shine tomorrow and I look forward to hearing about your day."

---

[5]　To learn how to do the 6-minute Miracle Morning, go to www.TMMAgents.com.

Rick and Michelle looked at each other and as both bounded towards the door to head to the shower, they ran right into each other. It wasn't enough to cause any damage, but they both laughed, and Rick instinctually wrapped his arms around her, squeezing her tightly. *How long has it been since we hugged and it felt this good?*

Just then, Rick's phone buzzed. After two vibrating rings, it was about to fall off the nightstand. Rick reluctantly let Michelle go and grabbed the phone.

He listened for a few moments, looked at Michelle, and while trying to keep his voice calm, said, "I've got to go to the office."

— 6 —

WHY SUCCESSFUL PEOPLE TALK TO THEMSELVES

Rick walked in and by the look on the face of Lisa, the office receptionist, he knew the entire office was aware of the news.

Damion and Denay were gone. *Betrayal.*

They didn't go empty-handed. In the dark of the night, they had also taken his entire database of past clients and leads, copied all his systems and documents, and tried to take Vanessa as well.

Vanessa was loyal. She stayed.

Rick looked around the office as if reviewing a crime scene. He couldn't believe it. He felt deceived. He felt violated. He could feel the blood rushing to his face. He left the office and went into the stairwell, slamming the door behind him. He had never felt such anger. *I will destroy them!* He punched the cement wall with his fist.

"OW!" he yelled, regretting his choice almost immediately. He slumped against the wall. Shaking his hand, he sighed heavily. *I'm done. My business can't survive this. I can't do this.* Rick took in a deep breath as Coach had instructed this morning. He saw someone pass the door obviously having heard him. He stood up, gathered himself, and headed back to the office.

Vanessa brought him a glass of water.

"Rick?" Vanessa said. "Rick!" she said a little louder looking at his now-swelling hand. "Are you okay?"

"I'm fine," Rick said. *I'm not fine. I just lost half my team! My partner and my top operations person.*

"I'll grab you some ice for your hand," Vanessa said, obviously concerned.

Rick felt sick.

"You look sick, sir," said a young man who turned the corner in front of Rick's office.

"I'm fine. Thank you," Rick said meekly.

"Wait a second," the young man said. "You're Rick Masters, aren't you? THE Rick Masters? You're in our office? I didn't know that."

Rick looked up.

The young man extended his hand and said, "I'm Jefferson Andrews. I'm a new agent here in the office. I've heard so much about you. It's, uhh... it's a pleasure to meet you, sir."

Rick mustered up as much enthusiasm as he could, and shook Jefferson's hand, trying to keep his pained grimace hidden.

Vanessa appeared with the ice. "Rick, I know you are upset, but we just got a call on River Oak Road and they want to see it TONIGHT," she said.

"Okay, I'll show it," Rick said meekly.

"Rick, you can't," Vanessa said. "I already had a listing appointment set up for Damion and I'm guessing you'd rather go to that than let Damion go. I've alerted the seller that it would be you and not Damion and they were excited."

Rick thought his head was going to explode.

"Perhaps I can help," Jefferson interjected.

Rick looked at Jefferson, looked at Vanessa, and then back to Jefferson.

"Sir, don't worry about pay," Jefferson said reading the look on Rick's face. "It will be my pleasure to show this couple the home on River Oak Road and do my best at converting them to a client for you."

"Wow," Rick replied. "Thank you Jefferson. That is very generous of you. Vanessa will get the information to you."

Don Dasick walked by, smirked, and shook his head slowly. *Know-it-all!*

Rick sighed heavily and looked around the office. *Where do I start?*

Miracle Morning Call #2

"Hello agents! Time to rise and shine! Are you ready to rock and roll? Today, 'A' in *Life SAVERS* is for Affirmations!" hollered Coach enthusiastically.

Michelle looked at Rick. Rick looked like death warmed over. *Rock and roll over in my grave, maybe.*

"Did you sleep at all?" Michelle asked while placing a steaming cup of coffee in front of him.

"Not much. I don't know if I could feel worse," Rick said.

"I am the greatest!" Coach said loudly. "Muhammad Ali affirmed these words over and over again—until he became them. Affirmations are one of the most effective tools for quickly programming your mind to become the person you need to be to achieve everything you want in your life. Affirmations allow you to design and then develop the mindset that you need to take any area of your life to the next level.

"It is no coincidence that some of the most successful people in our society—celebrities like Will Smith, Jim Carrey, Suze Orman, Muhammad Ali, Oprah, and many more—have all been vocal about their belief that positive thinking and the use of affirmations has helped them on their journey to success and wealth.

"Every single one of us has an internal dialogue that runs through our heads, almost non-stop. Most of it is unconscious, that is, we don't consciously choose the dialogue. Instead, we allow our past experiences—both good and bad—to replay over and over again. Not only is this completely normal, it is one of the most important processes for each of us to learn about and master. Yet, very few people take responsibility for actively choosing to think positive, proactive thoughts that add value to their lives, and take them where they want to go.

"I recently read a statistic that 80% of women have negative thoughts about themselves - about their body image, job performance, other people's opinion of them - throughout the day. I'm sure that men do also, although it may be to a lesser extent."

Rick looked at Michelle. She was nodding in agreement at what Coach said. She was writing on her page with her right hand and rubbing her midsection with her left hand. *She's thinking about the baby. I'm going to be a father.* Rick shook his head. *Oh my God! I'm going to be a dad!*

Coach continued, "Your self-talk has a dramatic influence on your level of success in every aspect of your life—confidence, health, happiness, wealth, relationships, etc. Your self-talk is either working for or against you, depending on how you are using it. If you don't consciously design and choose your affirmations, you are susceptible to repeating and reliving the fears, insecurities, and limitations of your past.

"However, when you actively design and write out your affirmations to be in alignment with what you want to accomplish and who you need to be to accomplish it—and commit to repeating them daily, ideally out loud - they immediately make an impression on your subconscious mind. Your affirmations go to work to transform the way you think and feel so you can overcome your limiting beliefs and behaviors and replace them with those you need to succeed."

Coach added, "Now, I will say that I believe there is a much more effective way to do affirmations than has been taught by countless experts and gurus throughout the years. You may have heard the traditional thinking that says affirmations should begin with 'I am' statements and follow with whatever it is that you want to be. *I am a millionaire. I am thin. I am successful.* While this can be effective, our research has shown that there is a better way.

"See, if you affirm *I am* _____, but the reality is that you're *not* whatever you're telling yourself that you are, then your subconscious mind is not going to believe you. Simply put, your affirmations aren't going to be effective when you don't believe them, because they're not true.

"Instead, the most effective way to phrase your affirmations is with 'I am committed to' statements, and then follow them up with a specific, measurable action, your ideal result, and a time frame. So, the Miracle Morning Affirmation formula is *I am committed to doing _____ NO MATTER WHAT so that I can _____ by _____. I am committed to doing 20 prospecting calls a day NO MATTER WHAT so that I can earn $200,000 by the end of this year. I am committed to doing 30 minutes of exercise everyday NO MATTER WHAT so that I can lose 20 pounds by December 31st.*

"You see, now you're programming your subconscious mind to do what you need to do to achieve the result you want, by the time you want to achieve it. You're reinforcing your level of NO MATTER WHAT commitment. With daily repetition, that is how affirmations can transform your mindset, thinking, and RESULTS.

"Take a minute now to follow this format and write your first three affirmations in your 30-Day Challenge Fast-Start Kit: *I am committed to doing _____ NO MATTER WHAT so that I can _____ by _____,*" instructed Coach. "Not all affirmations have to start with this phrase, but it will get you started. Do this now, and then I will tell you how affirmations changed my life. And remember, you can also get sample affirmations to customize for each area of your life at Error! Hyperlink reference not valid.

Rick and Michelle stared at their pages and then started writing. They were both very familiar with affirmations and writing them, but they had fallen from the habit over time.

Rick wrote, "I am committed to…" He stopped and thought. He hadn't realized the power of those four words and what follows. He thought about what to write. He thought of phrases like 'I am committed to being a top producer. I am committed to being a mega agent. I am committed to being the most successful agent in my market.' He could write them, but he didn't *feel* them. He felt like writing, 'I am tired. I am a bozo. I am not up to this. I feel like a loser.'

He gave it the college try.

Rick wrote:

"I am committed to re-building my team THIS WEEK NO MATTER WHAT, so that I am supporting my family.

"I am committed to getting up early and doing The Miracle Morning every day NO MATTER WHAT, so that I can become the person I need to be to create the life I deserve, both for me and my family, NOW.

"I am committed to implementing the follow up system I read in the book, (7L) *The Seven Levels of Communication* THIS WEEK, NO MATTER WHAT, so that I can rebuild my real estate business and get my income back where to where it needs to be.

"I am committed to buying and reading a book on how to be a great dad, today, NO MATTER WHAT so that I am ready to provide our child with the guidance he or she deserves.

"I am committed to exercising DAILY NO MATTER WHAT so that I am healthy, feeling great, and energized to do everything I want in life."

Rick wasn't sure if he was doing this right, but his new affirmations were already inspiring him to want to become the best version of himself. It felt as though reading affirmations everyday would remind him of what he really wanted, and more importantly, what he was committed to doing to earn, deserve, and create what he wanted. *Wow. This stuff is so powerful.*

How Affirmations Changed My Life

Coach shared, "My first real-life exposure to the power of affirmations came when I was in the military. I had a brother in arms, Chad Sanders. He owned a home a mile away from our base, and I rented a room from him.

"Nearly every day, I would hear Chad shouting from the shower in his bedroom. Thinking he was yelling for me, I would approach his bedroom door, only to find that he was shouting things like, 'I am in control of my destiny! I deserve to be a success! I am committed to doing everything I must do today to reach my goals and create the life of my dreams!' What a weirdo, I thought.

"Chad knew better. Chad had been using affirmations for years to create extraordinary levels of success. Owning five homes, and one of the top men in Special Forces, Chad was one of the most successful 25-year-olds I knew. I should have figured Chad knew what he was doing. After all, I was the one renting a room from him. Unfortunately, it took me a few more years to realize that affirmations were one of the most powerful tools for transforming your life.

"My first personal experience using affirmations came when I read about them in Napoleon Hill's legendary book, *Think and Grow Rich*. Although I was skeptical that the repetition of affirmations was really going to make any measurable impact on my life, I thought I would give it a shot. If it worked for Chad, it might work for me. I chose to target the limiting belief I had developed after suffering significant brain damage in a military bombing. Does that sound familiar? Like Rod, I suffered a severe concussion when my tank was jostled by bombing. On top of hitting my head and being knocked unconscious, I suffered some Post-Traumatic Stress Disorder. The result was having a horrible memory. Or should I say, I *had* a horrible memory," Coach corrected himself.

Coach continued telling his story. "As Henry Ford said, 'Whether you think you can, or you think you can't, you're right either way.' If affirmations could change what was, to me, the most justified limiting belief that I had, then they could probably change anything. So, I created my first affirmation, which was before I had learned the format I just taught you, but it was effective, nonetheless.

"It read: I am committed to letting go of the limiting belief that I have a horrible memory. My brain is an incredible organism capable of healing itself, and my memory can improve, but only in proportion to how much I believe it can improve. From this moment on, I am committed to maintaining the unwavering belief that my memory is continuing to improve and get better every day. Soon, my memory will be better than it's ever been!"

Rick stopped playing with his pen and listened intently to Coach's story. For some reason, Coach's affirmation triggered something in Rick. He felt goose bumps. *Could affirmations cure?*

Coach didn't hesitate. He said, "I read this short affirmation every day during my Miracle Morning. Still programmed with my past beliefs, I wasn't sure it was working. Then, two months after my first day reciting my affirmation, something occurred that hadn't occurred in over seven years. A friend asked me to remember to call her the next day, and I responded, 'Sure, no problem.' As soon as the words left my mouth, my eyes widened and I got excited! See, up until that point, I would have responded by saying, 'Sorry, I would. But I have brain damage.' But now, my limiting belief about my horrible memory was losing its power. **I had replaced it and reprogrammed my subconscious mind with my new, empowering belief, using my affirmations. I believed I would remember, and I did!**

"From that point on, my memory continued to improve and I created affirmations for every area of my life that I wanted to advance. I began using affirmations to improve my health, finances, relationships, happiness, as well as any and all beliefs, mindsets and habits that needed an upgrade. Nothing was off limits. There are no limits!" Coach said with passion.

"I'm genuinely excited about your implementation of affirmations in your real estate business, because I have seen struggling average producers become wealthy top producers. I have seen newbies take the real estate world by storm - reciting their laminated affirmations in the shower each morning or re-writing them daily in their journals. I have seen the power of re-programming your subconscious with affirmations," Coach said, ending with passion and emphasis. He said firmly, "Re-visit your affirmations from above and FEEL them. **If you knew, without a doubt that what you wrote for an affirmation was what you would become, what would you write?"**

Powerful question.

How's Your Programming?

Coach continued with today's lesson on Affirmations. "We've all been programmed, at the sub-conscious level, to think, believe, and act the way we do. Our programming is a result of many influences, including what we have been told by others, what we have told ourselves, and all of our life experiences—both good and bad. Some of us have programming that makes it easy for us to be happy and successful, while others, possibly the majority, have programming that makes life difficult.

"So, the bad news is that if we don't actively change our programming, our potential will be crushed and our lives limited by the fears, insecurities, and limitations of our past. We must stop letting the programming of our past keep us living a life of mediocrity. Remember, mediocrity isn't about how you compare to others. It's about who you are, compared to the person you know you can become. We program ourselves for mediocrity by focusing on what we're doing wrong, being too hard on ourselves when we make mistakes, and causing ourselves to feel guilty, inadequate, and undeserving of the success we really want…

"The good news is that our programming can be changed or improved at any time. We can reprogram ourselves to overcome all of our fears, insecurities, bad habits, and any self-limiting behaviors we currently have, so we can become successful. You can use affirmations to start programming yourself to be confident and successful in everything you do, simply by repeatedly telling yourself who you want to be, what you want to accomplish and how you are going to accomplish it. With enough repetition, your sub-conscious mind will begin to believe what you tell it, act upon it, and eventually manifest it in your reality," said Coach. Then he paused and made a point that Rick would remember forever.

"Listen to others. Talk to yourself," Coach said. "Listening to others, being a great listener, and learning from others, will catapult your relationships and life. But quit listening to yourself. Instead, talk to yourself. When you listen to yourself, you are hearing voices of the past, many of these program you to 'stop,' 'don't,' and 'no.' When you talk to yourself, you reprogram yourself to take action, establish great habits, and change behaviors to take your potential and make it your reality."

Rick wrote, "Listen to others. Be a great listener. Talk to yourself using positive self-talk and affirmations." *What is this? I feel motivated. Energized. Even with the lack of sleep and things happening to me right now, I am feeling energy. I am ready to take on these challenges. I am ready to take on the world.* Rick smiled when he realized he had just had a positive, affirming thought. Michelle noticed his smile and smiled warmly back.

"Don't just have affirming thoughts and talk to yourself," Coach continued. **"Your affirmations must be in writing.** And don't type them, physically write them down. Brain researchers have discovered that when you physically write, you are firing sparks in your brain. In essence, the grooves your pen is making into paper are also making grooves in your brain. Also, putting your affirmations in writing lets you review them often. That constant repetition will lead to acceptance and change in your mind. Acceptance by the mind will result in changes in your thoughts, beliefs and behaviors. Since you get to choose and create your affirmations, you can design them to help you establish the thoughts, beliefs, and behaviors that you want and need to succeed.

"Now, take a moment and review the sheet that came in your 30-Day Challenge Fast-Start Kit entitled, *The 5 Simple Steps to Create Your Own Affirmations.* Remember, everyone, go to **www. TMMAgents.com** to download sample affirmations that you can use to help you improve each area of your life. Let's read this together," Coach instructed.

Rick and Michelle pulled out the sheet and read:

The 5 Simple Steps to Create Your Own Affirmations
Step 1: What You Really Want

"What do you REALLY want?" Coach asked. Rick stared at his sheet. He looked at Michelle. He looked at her midsection. He took in a deep breath.

Coach hesitated for a second to let the force of that question sink in and then continued, "The purpose of a written affirmation is to program - even re-program - your mind with the beliefs, attitudes, behaviors, and habits that are vital to your being able to attract, create, and to sustain your ideal levels of success — Level 10 success —in every area of your life. *So, your affirmation must clearly articulate exactly what you want your ideal life to be like, in each area.*

"You can organize your affirmations according to the areas that you most want to focus on improving, such as Health/Fitness, Mindset, Emotions, Finances, Relationships, Spirituality, etc. Begin with clarifying, in writing, what you really want—your ideal vision for yourself and your life—in each area," Coach ended, with emphasis.

Rick shook his head. *What is my ideal vision for myself and my life?* He looked at Michelle. *I want an awesome life for my child and for my wife. I need to get it together.*

Step 2: Why You Want It

Rick and Michelle could hear Coach take a sip of a drink before starting again. "Everyone wants to be happy, healthy, and successful, but wanting is rarely an effective strategy for getting. Those who overcome the temptations of mediocrity and achieve everything they want in life have an extraordinarily compelling 'why' that drives them. They have defined a clear life purpose that is more powerful than the collective sum of their petty problems and the countless obstacles they will inevitably face. They wake up each day and work towards their purpose.

"Include why, at the deepest level, all of the things you want are important to you. Being crystal clear on your deepest desires will give you an unstoppable purpose," Coach said. "Now, recalling what you just wrote about what you really want, take a few moments to answer this question: what is important about getting what you really want? If you wrote, 'I want financial freedom' then answer, what is important about financial freedom to you? Go."

Rick tapped his pen on the pad of paper. *What is important to me about providing an awesome life for my family? Everything? It's important to me because I love them. I want my wife to not worry so much and I want my child to have an even better life, full of more opportunities than I did.*

Step 3: Who Are You Committed to Being to Create What You Want?

Coach said, "Commit to being better. **Your life gets better only after you get better.** Your outer world improves only after you've invested countless hours improving yourself. Being (who you need to be) and doing (what you need to do) are prerequisites for having what you want to have. Get clear on who you need to be, are committed to being, in order to take your life, business, health, marriage, etc. to the next level and beyond.

"When it comes to Physical, Intellectual, Emotional, and Spiritual realms in your life, what are you committing to being so that you can fulfill your want? What is your Spiritual Plan, your Health Plan, your Financial Plan, and your Growth Plan? Take care of you. Then you can take care of those around you."

Spiritual? Health? Financial? Growth? Rick stared at the blanks in his 30-Day Challenge Kit. He didn't know what his plan was for the rest of the day. He sat there thinking. *Which do I start with?*

Step 4: What You Are Committed To Doing To Attain It

"Commitment. Such a strong word," Coach said a few moments later. "Commit to doing better. Which actions will you need to take, on a consistent basis - commit to - to make your vision for your ideal life a reality? Want to lose weight? Your affirmation might be something like: 'I am 100% committed to going to the gym five days a week and running on the treadmill for a minimum of 20 minutes.' If you're a salesperson, your affirmation might read: 'I am committed to making 20 prospecting calls every day, from 8am-9am.' The more specific your actions are, the better. Be sure to include frequency (how often), quantity (how many), and precise time frames (what times you'll begin and end your activities.)."

"Write down an affirmation to show your commitment," Coach said.

Michelle quickly took pen to paper. Rick stared at his sheet in silence. His brain was done. He started to feel irritable. He started tapping his pen on his page.

Coach resumed, "It's also important to start small. If you're going to the gym zero days a week for zero minutes, jumping to five days a week for 20 minutes is a big leap. It's important to take manageable steps. Feel small successes along the way so you feel good and don't get discouraged by setting expectations too high to be able to maintain. You can build up to your ideal goal. Start by writing down a daily or weekly goal and decide when you will increase it. After a few weeks of successfully meeting your goal of going to the gym two-days-a-week for 20 minutes, then move it up to three-days-a-week for 20 minutes, and so on. Commit. Start small. Celebrate your successes. Now, let's go from celebrating to celebrities…"

Step 5: Add Inspirational Quotes and Philosophies

"Rick!" Michelle shouted. "Stop with the pen please." Rick stopped tapping his pen. His mind was starting to fill with things he needed to get done.

Coach continued, "I am always on the lookout for quotes and philosophies that I can add to my affirmations. For example, one of my affirmations comes from the book, *What Got You Here Won't Get You There* by Marshal Goldsmith. It reads, **'The #1 skill of influencers is the sincere effort to make a person feel that he or she is the most important person in the world.** It's one of the skills that Bill Clinton, Oprah Winfrey, and Bruce Goodman used to become the best in their fields. I will do this for every person I connect with!'

"Another reads: 'Follow Tim Ferriss' advice in *The 4-Hour Workweek*: To maximize productivity, schedule three to five hour blocks or half-days of singularly focused attention on ONE single activity or project, rather than trying to switch tasks every 60 minutes.' Gary Keller and Jay Papasan also talk about the power of this singular focus in their *New York Times* bestseller, *The ONE Thing*.

"Anytime you see or hear a quote that inspires you, jot it down and add it to your affirmations," Coach encouraged.

Final Thoughts on Affirmations

"There are five final things I have to say about Affirmations," Coach went into his closing. Rick gave a heavy sigh. *Oh, thank God. But five, really—in addition to what you've already said?* Rick stood up and started pacing. Michelle took notice for a moment, got ready to say something, thought better of it, and continued writing her notes.

"First, in order for your affirmations to be effective, it is important that you tap into your emotions while reading them. Mindlessly repeating a phrase over and over again, without feeling its truth, will have a minimal impact on you. You must take responsibility for generating authentic emotions and powerfully infusing those emotions into every affirmation you repeat to yourself. **Have fun with feeling it.** If you're excited about an affirmation, it doesn't hurt to dance and shout it from the rooftops!" Coach instructed. Rick kept pacing. *I need to get things done.*

"Second, it can also be beneficial to incorporate a purposeful physiology, such as reciting your affirmations while standing tall, taking deep breaths, making a fist, or even exercising. Combining physical activity with affirmations is a great way to harness the power of the mind-body connection. Writing and re-writing them also helps. Remember what Tony Robbins has been teaching us for decades, 'motion creates emotion,'" Coach added. Rick took a deep breath, grunting in pain after trying to make a fist with his hand. His hand was still swollen and bruised.

"Next, please keep in mind that your affirmations are always a work in progress. Your affirmations will never really be a 'final' draft, because you should always be updating them. **As you continue to learn, grow, and evolve, so should your affirmations.** When you come up with a new goal, dream, habit, or philosophy you want to integrate into your life, add it to your affirmations. When you accomplish a goal or completely integrate a new habit into your life, you might find it's no longer necessary to focus on it every day, and thus choose to remove it from your affirmations.

"Also, and this is very important, you must be consistent with reading your affirmations, daily. That's right, **you must read your affirmations daily**. Saying an occasional affirmation is as effective as getting an occasional workout. You won't see any measurable results until you make them a part of your daily routine. *That's largely what The Miracle Morning 30-Day Challenge is all about - creating daily habits of self-improvement,"* Coach emphasized.

"Finally, books, **reading and listening to books, is a form of an affirmation**. Anything you read influences your thoughts. When you consistently read and listen to positive self-improvement books and articles, you are programming your mind with the thoughts and beliefs that will support you in creating success." Rick nodded, still pacing. *Okay.*

Coach chuckled and concluded the day's lesson. "I am committed to ending our calls on time. I appreciate your time. I am fantastic at ending these calls on time. And… with… that… I am finished. Over and out everyone, see you tomorrow!"

Rick looked at the clock. Coach had ended at exactly the ending time. *Thank God! I am so antsy! I have to get out of here!*

Rick Takes a Walk

He had to get out of the house. He had to get some fresh air.

He started walking. He felt something was changing. He felt EVERYTHING was changing. Getting up in the morning, having to re-build his team, having to re-build his business, a new baby, a new beginning with Michelle. It was all so overwhelming. He had so much to do and felt an intense time crunch with the new baby only being a few months away, the leads coming in to him and only him, and Michelle not being able to work when the baby comes. His walking pace quickened and then he started jogging.

Taking mental inventory of his body, he was surprised at how good he felt considering he was without sleep and this was his first time jogging, or any exercise for that matter, in a long time.

I am doing okay.

He chuckled. *I think I just affirmed. I've set my bar so high that 'doing okay' is affirming.* He shook his head, took a deep breath, and continued his jog.

Every so often he thought of how he was feeling physically. He was surprised that he felt pretty good. His mind ran through the recent events. The baby, the conference, the coaching, the team, the new guy... *Okay, I've got this. One step at a time.*

Rick didn't know how far he had jogged. He looked around and realized that his journey had circled him back to the walkway to his home. He had gone several miles. He wiped his forehead. The sweat felt good. He was out of breath and his legs were rubbery but it felt good. The run felt good.

The New Guy

Rick showered and went to the office. He was one of the first ones to arrive. He looked at his phone and took a second to acknowledge all that he had already accomplished today - before most agents were even awake.

Upon entering the office, Rick noticed that something wasn't right with Lisa. From the concerned look on her face, Rick felt he needed to reassure her.

"Everything will be fine. Everything will be better than fine, Lisa," Rick said to her. As he said it, he noticed that they weren't just words to him. He meant it. He knew it. *It will be fine. I will be fine. We will be fine.*

Rick turned the corner to his office and there stood Jefferson. *Looking sharp, Jefferson!*

"Good morning, Jefferson," Rick greeted Jefferson with a smile.

"Good morning, Mr. Masters," Jefferson responded.

"Please call me Rick."

"Yes, sir," Jefferson replied.

"And no more 'sir,' understood?"

"Yes, s—, er, I mean, yes," Jefferson responded, catching himself. He smiled. "Mist-, er, I mean, Rick, I just want you to know that I've followed your success and really admire what you've done."

"Thank you, Jefferson," Rick said, feeling a little uncomfortable. "How did the River Oak Road showing go last night? You know what, before you answer that, let's go grab some coffee and I want you to tell me about what you did this morning before coming to the office."

7

THE POWER OF VISUALIZATION: SEE IT TO BELIEVE IT

Rick heard his alarm. He rolled over and instantly regretted it. He felt like he had been in a car wreck. His entire body had rebelled from yesterday's run. Every muscle in his body, even his neck, was sore. He could barely move. He tried putting the pillow over his head to drown out the alarm, but it was no use.

"Michelle!" Rick yelled, hoping she would turn off the alarm. *Why did I pick such an annoying sound for an alarm?*

After getting no answer, he realized that he was going to have to make it to the bathroom to turn off the alarm. He rolled over, trying not to bend any joint in his body. He misjudged how close he was to the edge of the bed, and with a loud thud, Rick hit the floor. *Well, I'm up now.*

Seeing Precedes Believing

"Time to rise and shine, agents!" Coach started the morning with his upbeat voice. "The 'V' in S.A.V.E.R.S. stands for Visualization and visualizing what 'shining' means to you can accelerate your success." *What does it mean for me to shine?*

Coach said, "Visualization, also known as creative visualization or mental rehearsal, refers to the practice of seeking to generate positive results in your outer world by using your imagination to create mental pictures of specific behaviors and outcomes occurring in your life. Frequently used by athletes to enhance their performance, visualization is the process of imagining exactly what you want to achieve or attain, and then mentally rehearsing what you'll need to do to achieve or attain it. Any question about what defines visualization?"

The agents responded with a chorus of "no's."

Coach kept going. "Many highly successful individuals, including celebrities, have advocated the use of visualization, claiming that it's played a significant role in their success - such successes include Bill Gates, Arnold Schwarzenegger, Anthony Robbins, and someone I've mentioned several times, Oprah.

"Tiger Woods, arguably the greatest golfer of all time, is famous for using visualization to mentally rehearse perfectly executing his golf swing on every hole. Another world champion golfer, Jack Nicklaus, has said: 'I never hit a shot, not even in practice, without having a very sharp in-focus picture of it in my head.'

"Will Smith stated that he used visualization to overcome challenges, and visualized his accomplishments years before becoming a success. Another famous example is actor Jim Carrey, who wrote himself a check in 1987 in the amount of $10 million. He dated it for 'Thanksgiving 1995' and added in the memo line, 'For acting services rendered.' He then visualized it for years, and in 1994 he was paid $10 million for his starring role in *Dumb and Dumber*," Coach said. "You don't have to be a celebrity or professional athlete to visualize. You can experience its power right now."

What Do You Visualize?

"Most people are limited by visions of their past, replaying previous failures and heartbreaks. Sometimes we visualize the future, but too often it's through a lens of fear or worry, thinking about what we might lose, or how we could fail.

"Miracle Morning Visualization enables you to design the ideal vision for your life, which will occupy your mind, ensuring that the greatest pull on you is your future - a compelling, exciting, and limitless future. First you see it, then you believe it, and then you create it. But it starts with creating your vision.

"I will say this: the traditional method of visualization is flawed," Coach warned. Rick's leaned forward. *Flawed?*

"As with traditional affirmations, the way visualization has been taught and practiced is not nearly as effective as it could be. Most experts have taught us to visualize the end result. They've instructed you to see yourself living in your mansion, driving your Ferrari, etcetera. This is a great start, but it is only half of the equation. It's far too easy to imagine this ideal life, feel good about it, and then go back to doing the same things you've always done, and getting the same results you've always got. I'm going to teach you the other half of the equation. It's a highly effective technique, which will turn your long-term vision into short-term action, so that your long-term vision becomes inevitable." *Inevitable?*

Coach took a sip of water and continued. "Here's how to do it...

"There are two parts to the Miracle Morning Visualization. After you've finished your Affirmations segment of S.A.V.E.R.S., sit upright on your chair, the floor, your living room couch, whatever is comfortable for you.

"The first part of your visualization will be focused on the long term, the big picture, by visualizing your most important goal or dream. The second half will be visualizing yourself actually doing the activities that you need to do TODAY, to ensure that your long-term vision becomes a reality.

"The experts have the **first part** of visualization correct; you visualize your ideal end result—what you really want that's important and meaningful to you. For example, when I was working on buying my dream home, I visualized what it would look like. I imagined myself walking through every room in the house, and I felt what it would feel like to own my dream home. This long-term visualization increases both your desire to make your vision a reality, as well as the belief that you can. As they say, seeing is believing, but you often have to see it before you start to believe it. You have to believe that it's possible.

"As I said a minute ago, it's far too easy to imagine this ideal life, feel good about it, and then go back to doing the same things you've always done, and getting the same results you've always gotten.

"The **second part** of visualization, the most important, life-changing aspect of it, is visualizing *short-term* actions. After you've spent a few minutes visualizing what you want for your future, now you've got to visualize yourself taking the necessary actions TODAY. And doing so with a smile on your face, with courage, and with a laser-like focus on your highest priorities. This is where visualization supports you in taking the necessary actions that will produce your desired results.

"I simply visualize myself living my ideal day, performing all of my tasks with ease, confidence, and enjoyment. I see the happy faces of those I meet with throughout the day. I see hour-by-hour my appointments and activities unfolding smoothly and easily. I also visualize bigger picture items. I visualize myself at my granddaughter's wedding, feeling healthy and strong, and dancing with her on this special occasion," Coach said whimsically.

Rick looked at Michelle. They didn't know what they were expecting - boy or girl. Rick could only imagine what it would feel like to be at his child's wedding, let alone their children's wedding. *What am I doing? I can't be thinking this way.* He gave himself a second to imagine himself at his daughter's wedding. He put his hand on his belly. *That's going to have to go.*

Three Simple Steps for Miracle Morning Visualization

"Okay, you've done your silence and you've just finished reading and perhaps writing your affirmations. Now is the prime time to visualize yourself living in alignment with your affirmations," Coach explained.

Step 1: Get Ready

"Some people like to play instrumental music in the background—such as classical or baroque, check out anything from the composer Bach, during their visualization. If you'd like to experiment with playing music, put it on with the volume relatively low.

Now, sit up tall, in a comfortable position. This can be on a chair, couch, floor, etc.

Breathe deeply.

Close your eyes, clear your mind, and get ready to visualize," Coach said. "Are you ready?"

Rick and Michelle both nodded.

Step 2: Visualize What You Really Want

"Many people don't feel comfortable visualizing success and are even scared to succeed. Some people may experience resistance in this area. Some may even feel guilty that they will leave the other 95% behind when they become successful.

"This famous quote from Marianne Williamson's bestselling book, *A Return To Love*, may resonate with anyone who feels mental or emotional obstacles when attempting to visualize:

> *'Our deepest fear is not that we are inadequate.*
> *Our deepest fear is that we are powerful beyond measure.*
> *It is our light, not our darkness that most frightens us.*
> *We ask ourselves,*
> *Who am I to be brilliant, gorgeous, talented, fabulous?*
> *Actually, who are you not to be?*
> *You are a child of God.*
> *Your playing small does not serve the world.*
> *There is nothing enlightened about shrinking so that other people*
> *won't feel insecure around you.*
> *We are all meant to shine, as children do.*
> *We were born to make manifest the glory of God that is within us.*
> *It's not just in some of us; it's in everyone.*
> *And as we let our own light shine, we unconsciously give other people*
> *permission to do the same.*
> *As we are liberated from our own fear, our presence automatically*
> *liberates others.'*

Whoa. Rick had heard this poem before, but it was a long time ago. But hearing it from Coach today gave him chills.

Coach continued his lesson on Visualization. He said, "The greatest gift we can give to the people we love is to live to our full potential. What does that look like for you? What do you really want? Forget about logic, limits, and being practical. If you could have anything you wanted, do anything you wanted, and be anything you wanted, what would you have, what would you do, and what would you be?

"Visualize your major goals, deepest desires, and most exciting, would-totally-change-my-life-if-I-achieved-them dreams. See, feel, hear, touch, taste, and smell every detail of your vision. Involve all of your senses to maximize the effectiveness of your visualization. The more vivid you make your vision, the more compelled you'll be to take the necessary actions to make it a reality.

"The point is that you want to see yourself accomplishing what you set out to accomplish, and you want to experience how good it will feel to have followed through and achieved your goals," Coach explained softly. "What do you see? How does it make you feel?"

Rick had a surprising thought. *He was in the hospital. They were in the birthing room. He could smell the cleanliness of the room and see the brightness of the lights. Michelle was giving birth to a baby. It was going smoothly. There was Damion and Denay. What?* Rick opened his eyes and shook his head. *Man, I've got to work on this visualization thing.*

Step 3: Visualize Who You Need To Be and What You Need To Do

Coach explained the third step about how to visualize. He instructed, "Once you've created a clear mental picture of what you want, begin to visualize yourself living in total alignment with the person you need to be to achieve your vision. See yourself engaged in the positive actions you'll need to do each day. That could be exercising, studying, working, writing, making calls, sending emails, or something else for you.

"Just make sure your vision is of yourself *enjoying* the process. See yourself smiling as you're running on that treadmill or road, feeling empowered and filled with a sense of pride for your self-discipline to follow through. Picture the look of determination on your face as you confidently, persistently make those phone calls, work on that report, or finally take action and make progress on that project you've been putting off for far too long. Visualize your customers, colleagues, family, friends, and/or your spouse responding to your positive demeanor and optimistic outlook," Coach softly and slowly guided them through the process of visualization.

Final Thoughts on Visualization

"As for some final thoughts on visualization, I want to give you some helpful tips. Keep in mind that in addition to reading your affirmations every morning, ***doing this simple visualization process every day will turbo-charge the programming*** of your subconscious mind for success. You will begin to live in alignment with your ideal vision and make it a reality.

"Visualizing your goals and dreams is believed by some experts to attract your visions into your life. Whether or not you believe in the law of attraction, there are practical applications for visualization. When you visualize what you want, you stir up emotions that lift your spirits and pull you towards your vision. The more vividly you see what you want, and the more intensely you allow yourself to experience, *now*, the feelings you will feel once you've achieved your goal, the more you make the possibility of achieving it feel real.

"When you visualize daily, you will subconsciously and automatically begin to align your thoughts and feelings with your vision. This makes it easier to maintain the motivation you need to continue taking the necessary actions. Visualization can be a powerful aid to overcoming self-limiting habits such as procrastination, and to taking the actions necessary to achieve your goals," Coach summarized.

"Practice Silence, Affirmations, and Visualization and you will be conditioning your mind for success. You will quickly start to become the Level 10 person you need to be to create and live a Level 10 life. In fact, you will be amazed at what happens with consistent implementation of these three practices— even if you don't 100% believe it. By putting into play just the first 50% of the *Life SAVERS*, you will already see significant and pleasant change.

"Thank you for rising and shining, today, agents. The world needs you to be at your best! See you tomorrow!"

Michelle headed to the shower. Rick headed outside.

Rick's First Planned Run

Rick didn't like how his body felt after yesterday's walk and run. He was so sore he could barely walk. His back was stiff and his entire body, especially his legs, hurt so badly he contemplated not getting dressed and going to work. Putting on his clothes, especially his socks and shoes, was a painful venture — he could hardly move!

But he did it anyway. He liked what he experienced on the road. He wasn't a runner, but he started jogging anyway. He knew from working out in high school that if he kept moving, kept doing, kept running and working out, that the soreness would eventually go away.

The first few steps hurt like heck.

He loved the silence of the road. He recited his affirmations. In reciting them, he knew he needed to make them more powerful. He needed to feel them at a deeper level. He needed to make them more specific and he needed to use them in his business, for his health, and as a husband.

He contemplated this morning's lesson on visualization. Rick enjoyed the silence and the affirmations. He would have to work on the visualization.

Rick Builds His Team

A week later, Rick rushed into his favorite restaurant to meet Jefferson for lunch.

"Sorry I'm late, Jefferson," Rick apologized.

"It's okay, Rick. You're busy. I'm glad you could meet." Jefferson responded.

"So, did you write the five contracts I asked you to get done?" Rick asked.

"Yes," Jefferson answered. "I believe I'm ready for you to look at them and negotiate with me."

"Great!" Rick said. "These fake contracts will prepare you for the real thing."

"Well, that's good because I believe the couple who saw River Oak Run with me want to write up on another house we saw," Jefferson replied.

"Jefferson, you've spent a lot of time with this couple," Rick said. Jefferson nodded. "Why don't we make some financial arrangements to ensure you get paid when they close?"

"That would be terrific, Rick," Jefferson responded.

The waitress came by and took their drink and food orders. Rick was impressed that Jefferson ordered only a healthy side salad and a water. *That's healthy.* Rick wondered if he would have noticed that before he started affirming that he was a healthy eater and made great eating choices.

"Jefferson, I've been thinking," Rick said slowly, looking up to get a gauge on Jefferson's reaction. "Why don't you take over more of my buyers? Why don't you work with me and Vanessa and handle buyers for us? You could work with a few now and then more later based on how you do."

"That would be quite an honor," Jefferson said, smiling. "I'd love to." Rick was pleased Jefferson was so receptive and appreciative.

Rick and Jefferson spent the next hour eating and discussing the contracts Rick had him doing as practice. Rick was tough on him, but Jefferson was an eager learner.

The waitress slipped Rick a Post-It.

"Jefferson, I have to run," Rick said urgently. "If you'll take care of this with the waitress, I'll get the next one? Sound good? Thanks." Then he was gone.

Jefferson watched him leave, handed the waitress his credit card, and waited for her to return.

"Sir, this didn't go through," the waitress said softly. "I'm sorry. Do you have another one?"

"Try this one," Jefferson said.

After a few minutes, she returned. "Sorry, that one was declined as well."

"Shoot, what are my options?" Jefferson asked.

"We know Mr. Masters. We could call him," the waitress answered.

"No," Jefferson said. "Can I please talk to your manager?"

8

MORNING EXERCISE: START EVERY DAY AT A LEVEL 10

"" Time to rise and shine, agents! The 'E' in S.A.V.E.R.S. is for... Exercise!" Coach cheerfully exclaimed.

"Today, we are going to spend more time on Exercise as you should be hitting your stride with Silence, Affirmations, and Visualization at this point. Morning exercise[6] should be a staple in your daily rituals. When you exercise for even a few minutes every morning, it significantly boosts your energy, enhances your health, and improves self-confidence and emotional well-being. It also

---

6   Legal disclaimer: Hopefully this goes without saying, but you should consult your doctor or physician before beginning any exercise regimen, especially if you are experiencing any physical pain, discomfort, disabilities, etc. You may need to modify or even refrain from your exercise routine to meet your individual needs.

enables you to think better and concentrate longer by increasing the flow of blood and oxygen to your brain. Still think you're too busy for exercise?"

Michelle touched the mute button and leaned over to Rick and whispered, "Do you feel ahead of the game, now that you're running?"

Rick nodded, liking that she'd noticed.

Coach continued, "I recently saw an eye-opening video with personal development expert and self-made multi-millionaire entrepreneur, Eben Pagan, who was being interviewed by world famous trainer and bestselling author, Anthony Robbins. Tony asked, 'Eben, what is your #1 key to success?' Of course, I was very encouraged when Eben's response was, **'Start every morning off with a personal success ritual. That is the most important key to success.'** He then went on to talk about the importance of morning exercise, saying, 'Every morning, you've got to get your heart rate up and get your blood flowing and fill your lungs with oxygen. Don't just exercise at the end of the day or at the middle of the day. And even if you do like to exercise at those times, always incorporate at least 10 to 20 minutes of jumping jacks or some sort of aerobic exercise in the morning.'

"In an interview, uber-entrepreneur and billionaire Sir Richard Branson was asked what someone should do to be more productive. He answered with two words, 'Work. Out.' The benefits of morning exercise are too many to ignore. From waking you up and enhancing your mental clarity, to helping you sustain higher levels of energy throughout the day, exercising soon after rising can improve your life in many ways.

"Whether you go to the gym, go for a walk or run, or throw on a workout DVD, what you do during your period of exercise is up to you, but **the benefits of *morning* exercise are undeniable and something you can't skip if you're committed to peak performance in your life and business**," Coach explained. "So, what would you like to do for 10-30 minutes in the morning, to get your heart rate up, increase blood flow, and release those mood-enhancing endorphins?"

Rick proudly and quickly wrote, "Run." Michelle was playing with her pen.

"You should ask your doctor what she suggests when it comes to exercise, sweetie," Rick said.

Michelle nodded. Rick could see she wrote her doctor's name and number down.

"Personally, and this may seem surprising coming from an ex-military man who grew up without exposure to yoga, but if I were only allowed to practice one form of exercise for the rest of my life, I would, without a doubt choose yoga.

"At first, I made fun of those practicing yoga, especially men. I know, I know, I was being completely close-minded. Then, I tried a beginner's class. It was called 'Yoga for the Stiff Guy.' Rick and Michelle chuckled and heard some laughs and snorts on the conference line. "—and trust me, I didn't tell anyone I was doing yoga. I noticed that the 'old man' feel I had been getting - creaks and pops in joints, moans getting out of chairs, and overall stiffness - wasn't about getting old, it was about being sedentary. It was due to a lack of flexibility."

"The more I practiced yoga; the younger I felt. It's such a complete form of exercise, as it combines stretching, strength training, cardio, focused breathing, and can even be a form of meditation."

Coach paused. "I don't want to seem like I am selling yoga - or any other type of exercise. What I am selling is the profound, life and business enhancing benefits of morning exercise in your life, not just for your body, but also for your mental and emotional well-being. And all of those benefits will contribute to benefiting your results and your bottom line!"

"You'll find your exercise plan in your 30-Day Challenge Kit," Coach said. "So decide what you will do for your morning exercise, each day - even if it is just for 5-10 minutes."

Final Thoughts on Exercise

Coach had a few minutes left before the session was finished so he put in a few final words about exercise. Obviously, this was a sensitive and passionate subject for Coach.

Coach said, "You know that if you want to maintain good health and increase your energy, you must exercise consistently. That's not news to anybody. But it's too easy to make excuses as to why we don't exercise. Two of the biggest are, 'I just don't have time' and 'I'm just too tired.' There is no limit to the excuses that you can think of. The more creative you are, the more excuses you can come up with, right?

"That's the beauty of incorporating exercise into your Miracle Morning 30-Day Challenge; it happens before your day wears you out, before you have a chance to get too tired, before you have an entire day to come up with new excuses for avoiding exercise. The Miracle Morning is really a surefire way to avoid all of those excuses, and to make exercise a daily habit. **If you think about it, without your health, what do you really have?"** Rick had to agree.

Rick Runs

Rick headed out the door to do his morning jog.

Michelle was right. He did feel ahead of this session because he started walking and jogging a week before the E for Exercise session. It felt good to be ahead. Even though he hadn't lost any weight, he did notice his energy was improved throughout the day and he no longer found himself out of breath from going up the stairs.

He turned the corner moving slowly, but steadily. As usual, he began thinking about his Miracle Morning and, of course, work.

The 30-Day Challenge had given him a sense of control over his day - a feeling he had never experienced before. He had really felt weird trying to be silent the first few days. And as Coach said, that is why they start with Silence. Rick still struggled, but he was enjoying the quiet mornings with Michelle and he was seeing progress in his demeanor. He felt calmer and more in control. A seller had even commented on it yesterday. He absolutely loved the affirmations and felt that many of the positive things that had happened to him in the last two weeks were due to his positive self-talk. The positive self-talk was making him more positive. *That makes sense.*

He was laboring a little bit but didn't stop. As he turned the second corner, he thought about Visualization. He noticed that during his Miracle Morning routine, he sometimes felt the urge to blast right past visualization. Every time he started to visualize, he tended to think about personal things - visualizing himself feeling light on his feet while jogging or visualizing a smooth delivery for Michelle. Coach had emailed him encouragement to start implementing visualization in small, but powerful ways at work - before a listing appointment, buyer consultation, phone call, and even before a networking event or One-on-One. He just needed to stop and make a point of doing it. He definitely still needed to work on this.

As he turned the last corner, he chugged along. His heart stepped up a beat when he thought of Damion and Denay's antics. They could have just told him they were leaving and left professionally. But to leave in the dark of the night AND take his database and Operations Manual was just infuriating. And then to top it off, Rick heard from an agent in his office that Damion had been badmouthing Rick and Vanessa. *What a jerk. Say all you want about me, but leave Vanessa out of it.*

His run was normally refreshing, but today he felt exhausted and wondered if it was all worth it. He grudgingly did his post-run stretching. As he did, a bus passed and what he read on the side of it jolted him in his shoes. He ran inside the house.

— 9 —

30-DAY CHALLENGE (WEEK 4): READ TO LEAD

Ripped Off

Michelle had gotten home late because of some client meetings and he couldn't wait to talk to her.

"I can't believe they are using MY numbers in their advertising!" Rick said as Michelle handed him his coffee. He hadn't slept much thinking about how to respond.

"How do you know those are your numbers?" Michelle asked.

"We were just reviewing these on a call last quarter," Rick answered shaking his head. "And as much as I've been out of the office, I know my numbers. Those are my sales-price-to-list-price percentages, number of sales, and average days on market. They were on the team, but Damion has never listed a property in his life!"

"I'm sorry, Rick," Michelle said sympathetically. "Hey, what do you think Coach would say about what you should do?"

Rick thought about it.

"He'd probably say to just stop, breathe, and meditate on it," he finally replied.

He felt calmer just saying it, but he was still angry. Had this happened before he started the 30-day Challenge, he probably would have driven like a maniac over to Damion's office and confronted him. *Am I getting soft? Am I losing my fire?*

R is for Reading

Rick noticed that other than his resentment towards Damion and Denay, he felt good. The first week of the 30-Day Challenge was almost unbearable and he noticed even Michelle who had been getting up early had some difficulty that week. Coach said it was going to be tough. The second week really felt more uncomfortable than unbearable. He wasn't mentally and physically resisting as much as the first week. It was more of an adjustment. Week three was solid. Rick and Michelle felt a sense of accomplishment. Now, he was starting to see the changes in his life from having embraced the Miracle Morning. He felt more powerful.

Coach definitely hadn't lost his fire. He was on today! Rick and Michelle could feel his passion through the phone.

"Hello Agents! Time to rise and shine! Today's topic may be my favorite!" Coach said. "The 'R' in S.A.V.E.R.S. is for Reading. Reading is the fast track to transforming any area of your life, personally or professionally. It is one of the most immediate methods for acquiring the knowledge, ideas, and strategies you need to achieve Level 10 success in any area. What was the last book you read? Please write the title in your 30-Day Challenge Fast-Start Kit."

Michelle took no time in writing her title. He knew she had written down the latest self-help title or perhaps a chapter in the Bible. Rick had to think for a while. He could think of some magazines and his news feeds on the Internet, but no book. Rick remembered the half-read book next to his bed. He went into the bedroom. Underneath the bed, he found the last book he had read. He opened it. *Correction, the last book I started.*

After a pause, Coach's energetic voice boomed again, "**There is very little difference between someone who is illiterate and someone who can read and yet doesn't.** And if you ask me, the second one is more pathetic! To have such a beautiful ability and not use it is an absolute atrocity."

Rick and Michelle looked at each other. "Whoa!" Michelle mouthed to Rick. Rick just shook his head in wonder. *Coach is bringing it today!*

"So many people are looking for the secret sauce or magic pill to success. Truth be told, the closest thing in the world to a magic pill is a book. Agents and brokers, books are the magic pill! Ingredients that can cure any challenge! All that passion, sweat, wisdom, heart, and soul that someone had to invest, possibly millions of dollars to acquire, and then years to hone, is rolled into one small package and sold for $20-30! Thirty dollars? What would you pay for 100 hours of Rod Halsten's time or Jay Michaels' time or Reece or Ken's time? And to be honest, it could be 10,000 hours or more as these guys are masters at their craft and mastery can take more than 10,000 hours. All those hours rolled into one thirty dollar package! Take advantage of that offer any time you can!" *Never thought about books like that!*

"The key is to learn from the experts—those who have already done what you want to do. Don't reinvent the wheel. The fastest way to achieve everything you want is to model successful people who have already achieved it. With an almost infinite amount of books available on every topic, there are no limits to the knowledge you can gain through daily reading," Coach said. "Can you tell I love reading and readers?" he chuckled.

Rick and Michelle laughed out loud. *So lucky to have Coach helping me with this.* Rick recognized that he was appreciative, and smiled to himself. This program was making him different, more appreciative and grateful.

"Whatever you want in life… or out of life… whether you'd like to transform your relationships, increase your self-confidence, improve your communication or persuasion skills, learn how to become wealthy, or improve any area of your life, head online or to a local bookstore and you'll find a variety of choices. For those who want to minimize our carbon footprint or save money, I also recommend utilizing your local library or checking out one of the many book-swapping Web sites," Coach suggested.

"You can download a list of Rod's favorite books for improving any area of your life, at **www.TMMAgents.com.**

Readers are Leaders

"Okay, commitment time," Coach said. "Your commitment is to read a minimum of ten pages per day. We're only talking 10-15 minutes of reading, or 15-30 minutes if you read more slowly. But look at it this way: reading just ten pages a day will average 3,650 pages a year, which equates to approximately eighteen 200-page personal development/self-improvement books! Let me ask you, if you read eighteen personal development books in the next twelve months, do you think you will be more knowledgeable, capable and confident — a new and improved you? Absolutely! Aren't you excited about the potential - your potential? Just by reading ten pages per day! Do you see why I was so fired up during today's lesson?" *Coach has some good points. I am committing to read more.*

Reading and Re-reading

Coach started to wrap up but his energy hadn't ebbed.

"Agents, Dr. Stephen Covey once said, 'Begin with the end in mind.' The same should be said with your Reading Plan. Before you begin reading each day, ask yourself why you are reading that book and keep that outcome in mind. Also, I've been asked by others who made it this far in the 30-Day Challenge and I want to assure you that many Miracle Morning practitioners use their Reading time to catch up on religious texts, such as the Bible, Torah, or any other."

"You've written down the last book you read. Now, take a second and write down the name of the book you will be reading from now on during your Miracle Morning 30-Day Challenge."

Rick quickly wrote down his choice of book. It was a fable. He liked books that incorporated stories to illustrate points. He knew without looking at Michelle's notes that she wrote down the Bible. *Perhaps that will be next for me.*

"Let me throw another thought out to you that may seem unusual," Coach said. "Plan for RE-READING. I highly recommend re-reading good personal development books. Rarely can we read a book once and internalize all the value from that book. Achieving mastery requires repetition—being exposed to certain ideas, strategies, or techniques over and over again, until they become engrained in the subconscious mind. For example, if you wanted to master karate, you wouldn't learn the techniques once and then think, 'I got this.' Would you?" Coach said.

Rick and Michelle shook their head.

"No," Coach continued, "you'd learn the techniques, practice them, then go back to your sensei and learn them again, and repeat the process hundreds of times in order to master a single technique.

Bruce Lee once said, 'I do not fear the man with 10,000 kicks. I fear the man who has practiced one kick 10,000 times.'"

"Mastering techniques to improve your life works the same way. There is more value in re-reading a book you already know has strategies that can improve your life than there is in reading a new book before you've mastered the strategies in the first," Coach paused to let that thought soak into the minds of the agents.

He then added, "Rod gave me a great suggestion. Whenever I'm reading a book that makes an impact on me, I commit to re-reading that book. I actually keep a special space on my bookshelf for the books that I want to re-read. Re-reading requires discipline, because it is typically more 'fun' to read a book you've never read before. Repetition can be boring or tedious - which is why so few people ever master anything. That's even more reason why we should commit to re-reading."

Re-reading is more powerful than reading, Rick committed to memory.

"Which reminds me of touring Jay Michael's library recently," Coach recalled. "Nearly every book in his library had colored Post-Its hanging out of them, folded corners, and some books he showed me had multiple colors of highlighting as well. Jay is not afraid to devour a book. I know Rod, Ken, and Reece are the same way."

"Look at your 30-Day Challenge Fast-Start Kit," Coach continued. "Have you been underlining, circling, highlighting, folding corners of pages, or taking notes in the margins? To get the most out of any book and make it easy to revisit the content again in the future, I suggest underlining or circling anything that you may want to re-visit. Make notes in the margins to remind yourself why you underlined that particular section. Using these techniques, you can quickly recapture the wisdom from the book."

"Ladies and gentlemen... agents, Realtors, and brokers... our call has come to a close. 'R' is for Reading. Readers are leaders and learners are earners. Attack your day with a dose of the magic pill - lessons from leaders and wisdom from the wise. Make it a great one!"

With that closing, the line went quiet. Rick and Michelle looked at each other. *Whoa.*

"Was Coach on fire today or what?" Rick asked Michelle.

"He was," Michelle replied. "I've never heard someone explain the power of reading so well. Are you going to start reading again? You read a lot of stuff - emails, Facebook, blogs, sports sites. Are you going to read books?"

"I'm in," Rick said. "I'm actually going to do as Coach said. I am going to re-read *(7L) The Seven Levels of Communication.*"

"Let's read it together," Michelle said.

"Awesome," Rick said enthusiastically and Michelle gave him a big hug. *Ooh, I like that. What just happened?*

Rick and Jefferson Run

This morning, Jefferson joined Rick for his run. Rick was glad he had been running because Jefferson was about 10 years younger and in great shape. Rick was surprised Jefferson started out so slow. As it turned out, he was more interested in talking than jogging.

"So what are you reading?" Jefferson asked.

"I am actually re-reading a book on real estate referrals," Rick replied. "It's a story and includes the system, strategies, and tactics. How about I get you a copy?"

"Wow, that would be great," Jefferson said, genuinely appreciative. "Rick, can I tell you something?"

Jefferson confessed about the lunch, not being able to even pay for a simple lunch. He was forced to sell some things to pay the restaurant back, pay his rent, and make ends meet.

"I really love real estate," Jefferson said. Rick silently jogged beside Jefferson. "I love the freedom, the helping people, and having you as a mentor is a dream come true. I am going to be great at real estate. I know I am, but— "

"Before you talk about whatever follows the 'but', let's jog for a few minutes in complete silence. I'm not mad at you and you don't even need to think about me - or anything else at all. Just feel your breath and the air, and just be still, be totally present to the running as if nothing else matters, and enjoy the silence for a few minutes. I'll break the silence when it's time, but for now, let's just tune into nothing," Rick said.

He wasn't entirely sure if he could both jog and talk for very long, so his advice wasn't given for purely unselfish reasons. They ran quietly for quite a while. In the beginning, Rick noticed Jefferson speed up his run, making Rick have to adjust his own pace. After a mile or so, Jefferson throttled down and both fell into a nice rhythm - not too slow and not too fast. They turned the final corner and stopped at Rick's place.

"What did you think about?" Rick asked. It felt good to stop. Even with the rhythm they had set, he wasn't ready for more than a few miles.

"At first, I thought of a million things," Jefferson said. Rick noticed that Jefferson was breathing hard as well. After catching his breath, he continued, "I thought of everything I needed to do, about money and not having any, and about you and what you wanted me to get out of this 'silence thing.' Then, I tuned into my breathing, like you told me to," Jefferson said. "I really didn't think of anything after that. Just enjoyed the run… just enjoyed being alive. I don't know, Rick. I can't really describe it."

"You can't really describe it, but you just did," Rick said. "Let's stretch a little and talk about what's next. You've cleared your mind. Now, let's fill it with good stuff - and just so you know, you've already started this process. We just need to tweak it a little."

"Okay," Jefferson replied.

"When you said, 'I am going to be great at real estate' you did what's called an affirmation," Rick said. "Affirmations are positive self-talk. I'm learning this in my Miracle Morning 30-Day Challenge. Something I learned was to put the affirmations into present tense, instead of future tense."

"What do you mean?" Jefferson asked, genuinely curious. *This kid's hungry. I like that.*

"Instead of saying, 'I am going to be,' you should say, 'I am committed to becoming.' So you would say, 'I am committed to becoming great at real estate,'" Rick taught.

"But I'm not great at real estate right now," Jefferson answered. *Good point.*

"You aren't but you will be. I can tell you are committed to becoming great at real estate. See it in the positive and it will happen more quickly," Rick answered. "I'll give you an example. I was absolutely, positively not a morning person. I'd hit snooze 11 - 12 times before getting up. I started saying an affirmation, 'I am committed to rising and shining no matter what! I rise and shine every day and win the day!' After a week or so, I noticed that my affirmation was coming true. Not only was I okay with getting up earlier, but I noticed that my day was full of shining - excelling, achieving, and productivity. And you know what? I just noticed something. I just said, 'I *wasn't* a morning person.' Ha! I guess I am a morning person now - and affirmations helped me change that mentally before it changed in reality. Whatever you want to have, do, and become, you must first speak into existence. First you say it, then you do it, and then you become it. Does that make sense?" Rick explained.

"Perfectly," Jefferson answered. "Is it really that simple?"

"Maybe," Rick replied. "Let's try one for you. What can we do an affirmation about for you?"

"'I am committed to becoming great at real estate' comes to mind," Jefferson answered.

"How would you know if you are great at real estate?" Rick asked.

Jefferson paused to think about it. They had finished stretching and the sweat was pouring off of both of them.

"How would I know if I was great at real estate?" Jefferson repeated Rick's question. "I would be getting referrals from everyone I know. If you are great at real estate, like you, people who know you would send their friends to you and call you when they needed real estate help. Right?"

"Absolutely," Rick said, smiling. "So create an affirmation."

"I am committed to receiving referrals from everyone I know?" Jefferson said hesitantly.

"Good," Rick said. Then taking a lesson he learned from Coach on the 30-Day Challenge calls, he said, "Now, say it with more authority, by adding 'no matter what.' Feel it. Feel it to be true."

"I AM committed to receiving referrals from everyone I know NO MATTER WHAT!" Jefferson said with more authority. He smiled. "It feels good to say. I think I'm getting this."

"It took me a while at first. We'll tweak it later by adding a timeline. But that's good for now, 'cause I need to run," Rick replied, smiling.

"Oh, okay, thanks again Rick!" Jefferson said with enthusiasm. "I'll see you at the office."

"I AM committed to receiving referrals from everyone I know TODAY NO MATTER WHAT!" Jefferson said to himself as he was walking off.

Rick smiled, but it immediately faded as he walked in to see Michelle writhing in pain on the floor of their kitchen.

— 10 —

THE FINAL 'S' OF THE LIFE S.A.V.E.R.S.

Rick held Michelle's hand.

After the frantic trip through traffic to the emergency room, Michelle had been admitted and they were waiting on their doctor. Michelle had spotted some blood and was suffering from extremely painful cramps. He could feel her squeeze his hand when the pangs shot through her.

"I am going to be fine," Michelle reassured Rick.

"I love that affirmation," Rick replied, obviously concerned. "When I saw you on the floor, my heart sunk to the bottom of my stomach."

"I hope everything is fine with the baby," Michelle said, rubbing her stomach. Rick put his hand on her hand and nodded soberly.

"Me too," he said softly.

The doctor walked in. "The baby is fine. You are going to be fine," she said. Her quick entry jolted Rick out of his seat and startled Michelle. "Oh, sorry," their doctor replied. "I just rushed over from delivery when I got the page. Michelle, you need to stay off your feet for the next few days. We'll keep you here for the night to make sure all is okay, but all vital signs for the baby are good based on what the nurses did. You just need the rest. Have you been pushing yourself too hard?"

Michelle looked at Rick. *She needs me. She needs my help.*

"Perhaps," Michelle replied truthfully. *She needs to relax, take it easy.*

"Well, let's see what happens today," the doctor said. "Remember, you are making decisions and choices for two." *I need to make decisions for three.*

Rick kissed Michele on the forehead, asked her to take it easy, and headed to a day full of listing appointments and showings with a renewed purpose. *Today, it is about my family. That's my why.*

Rick had a terrific day, even refusing to take 'no' from a seller about lowering the price of their house. He knew that it was in the seller's best interest and the house had a better chance to sell at the lower price. The seller agreed to lower the price and on the way back to the hospital an agent called him to get permission to show the next morning.

Michelle was sleeping, peacefully like an angel when he arrived. Arranging a chair next to the bed, Rick got comfortable and gently slipped his hand inside hers.

Miracle Morning in the Hospital

The next morning, Rick opened his eyes to see Michelle staring at him. He could see the love in her eyes.

"Good morning," he said.

"Good morning," she croaked. "Thirsty." She smiled. Rick got up and got them each a cup of water. Both had been drinking lots of water and starting their day with a tall glass of water based on Coach's suggestion.

They had been doing the Miracle Morning rituals at the same time, but separately. Today was the first time in a few weeks they did it together. In Silence, Rick felt a wave of gratitude and love for Michele that he had not felt since the first time they dated.

What would I do if I lost her? He shook his head as if to get that thought out of his head.

Today, as they spoke their Affirmations together, he felt more passion, more power, and more commitment than ever before. And he added one based on Michelle's affirmations. She said with conviction, "I am committed to being a supermom. I am committed to raising my child to be a blessing." Rick added, "I am committed to being the best dad in the world. I am committed to raising my child to be successful."

During Visualization, Rick visualized the birth of his child - for some reason a boy came to mind. He was there for Michelle and it was smooth and as pain-free as possible. Rick felt an anxious moment. *God, tell me the baby is okay. Keep our baby healthy. Keep Michelle healthy.*

He knew he was going to run later so, Michelle read a book on being a new mom, and Rick read his book on referrals. *Feels better to stay with the ritual.*

The Final 'S' In S.A.V.E.R.S.

Before they knew it, it was time for the call. Rick and Michelle dialed into their Miracle Morning 30-Day Challenge Call from the hospital room. Coach jumped right in with the day's lesson.

"We needed a word that means 'writing' and started with an S to complete the SAVERS acronym," Coach said. "So, thanks to the thesaurus, Scribing is the final practice in the Life SAVERS," he laughed. Rick and Michelle both laughed as well.

Coach continued, "We encourage you to not just find time for Silence, Affirmations, Visualizations, Exercise, and Reading… but to also write, preferably in a journal. Journaling is essentially writing on your brain. One of the best ways to learn is to write."

Journaling

"By getting your thoughts out of your head and putting them in writing, you gain valuable insights. The Scribing element of your Miracle Morning enables you to document your insights, ideas, breakthroughs, realizations, successes, and lessons learned, as well as any areas of opportunity, and personal growth or improvement. It also allows you to prioritize your daily activities and reinforce your daily commitments, in writing.

"Let me tell you my experience with journaling. Perhaps you can relate," Coach said. Rick always liked it when Coach was completely open and willing to share his experiences with implementing these self-improvement habits.

"While I had known about the profound benefits of journaling for years—and I had even tried it a few times—I never stuck with it consistently, because it was never part of my daily routine. Usually, I kept a journal by my bed, and when I'd get home late at night, nine times out of ten I would find myself making the excuse that I was too tired to write in it. My journals stayed mostly blank. And get this… even though I already had many mostly blank journals sitting on my bookshelf, every so often I would buy myself a brand new journal - a more expensive one - convincing myself that if I spent a significant amount of money on it, I would surely write in it. Seems like a decent theory, right? Unfortunately, my little strategy never worked, and for years I just accumulated more and more increasingly expensive, yet equally empty journals. Can anyone relate?" Coach asked.

A few "yeses" came through the phone.

Coach went on, "That was before *The Miracle Morning*. From day one, *The Miracle Morning* gave me the time and structure to write in my journal every day, and it quickly became one of my favorite habits. I can tell you now that journaling has become one of the most gratifying and fulfilling practices of my life. Not only do I derive the daily benefits of consciously directing my thoughts and putting them in writing, but even more powerful are those I have gained from reviewing my journals, from cover to cover, afterwards—especially, at the end of the year. It is hard to put into words how overwhelmingly constructive the experience of going back and reviewing your journals can be, but I'll do my best."

Looking Back to Propel Forward

Coach took a deep breath and Rick could hear him gathering some papers. Coach explained, "On December 31ˢᵗ, after my first year doing *The Miracle Morning* and writing in my journal, I began reading the first page I had written that year. Day-by-day, I started to review and *relive* my entire year. I was able to revisit my mindset from each day, and gain a new perspective as to how much I had grown throughout the year. I reexamined my actions, activities, and progress, giving me a new appreciation for how much I had accomplished during the past twelve months. Most importantly, I recaptured the lessons I had learned, many of which I had forgotten over the course of the year.

"I also experienced a much deeper quality of gratitude on two different levels. I was now looking back at all of the people, experiences, lessons, and accomplishments that I took note of being grateful for throughout the year. As I was in that moment reliving the gratitude that I felt in the past, I was simultaneously feeling grateful in the present moment for how far I had come since that time in my life. It was a remarkable experience, and a bit surreal. I do this every year and still get this feeling.

"Then, I began to tap into the highest point of value I would gain from reviewing my journals. I pulled out a sheet of blank paper, drew a line down the middle, and wrote two headings at the top: *Lessons Learned* and *New Commitments*. As I read through my hundreds of my journal entries, I found myself recapturing dozens of valuable lessons.

"This process of recapturing *Lessons Learned* and making *New Commitments* to implement those lessons, aided my personal growth and development more than almost anything else.

"While there are many worthwhile benefits of keeping a daily journal, a few of which I've just described, here are a few more of my favorites: You gain clarity, capture ideas, review lessons learned, and document your progress. You've been writing in your journal included in the Fast-Start Kit since we've started so you've experienced the power of journaling. What are some insights or some interesting discoveries you've found from writing?"

"Hello?" said someone on the line.

"Yes, go ahead," Coach said.

"This is Emmett, in LA," the voice said. "I have been writing since day one and I've noticed that being triggered by questions has helped a ton. While you were talking about reviewing what we wrote, I noticed that I've written a little bit more each day."

"Great stuff, Emmett," Coach encouraged. "Never feel constraints on your journal. You can write as much or as little as you wish. Some of you will use the journal as a catch-all for all your notes, ideas, affirmations, visualizations, and more. Some of you will just jot about specific topics. **We are here to encourage you to just develop the habit of journaling so you can find your inner scribe, so to speak.** This daily record will help you with what can be a destructive mindset, something called 'gap-focus.'"

Gap-Focus: Is It Hurting or Helping You?

"Another potential power of scribing and writing is dealing with something called 'gap-focus.' Rod introduced this concept to me and I have to say it is right on - especially his take on high achievers. We tend to focus on the gaps between where we are in life and where we want to be, between what we've accomplished and what we could have or want to accomplish; the gap between who we are and our idealistic vision of the person we believe we should be. The problem with this is that constant gap-focus can be detrimental to our confidence and self-image, causing us to feel like we don't have enough, haven't accomplished enough, and that we're simply not good enough, or at least, not as good as we should be." Rick and Michelle looked at each other and nodded. *That makes sense.*

"High achievers are typically the worst at this, constantly overlooking or minimizing their accomplishments, beating themselves up over every mistake and imperfection. They never feel like anything they do is quite good enough.

"The irony is that gap-focus is a big part of the reason that high achievers are high achievers. Their insatiable desire to close the gap is what fuels their pursuit of excellence and constantly drives them to achieve. Gap-focus can be healthy and productive if it comes from a positive, proactive perspective, without any feelings of lack. Unfortunately, it rarely does. The average person, even the average high achiever, tends to focus negatively on their gaps.

"The highest achievers, those who are balanced and focused on achieving *Level 10* success in nearly every area of their lives, are exceedingly grateful for what they have. They regularly acknowledge themselves for what they've accomplished, and are always at peace with where they are in their lives. It's the duel idea that **I am doing the best that I can in this moment,** and at the same time, **I can and will do better**. This balanced self-assessment prevents that feeling of lack, of not being, having, or doing enough, while still allowing them to constantly strive to close their potential gap in each area," Coach summarized. "Does this make sense to everyone?"

Many on the call agreed. Then, a soft voice said, "No."

Coach encouraged the person to speak up.

"This is Travis from Michigan," said the voice. "I'm a little confused. Can you give me an example of gap-focus and how this works?"

Coach's voice indicated that he was glad for the question. "Sure. Typically, when a day, week, month, or year ends, and we're in gap-focus mode, it's almost impossible to maintain an accurate assessment of ourselves and our progress. For example, if you had 10 things on your to-do list for the day, even if you completed six of them, your gap-focus causes you to feel you didn't get everything done that you wanted to do.

"The majority of people do dozens, even hundreds, of things right during the day, and a few things wrong. Guess which things people remember and replay in their minds over and over again? Doesn't it make more sense to focus on the 100 things you did right? It sure is more enjoyable.

"What does this have to do with writing in a journal? Writing in a journal each day, with a *structured*, strategic process - I will get to the structure here in a second - allows you to direct your focus to what you did accomplish, what you're grateful for, and what you're committed to doing better tomorrow. Thus, you more deeply enjoy your journey each day, feel good about any forward progress you made, and use a heightened level of clarity to accelerate your results. Does that make sense Travis - and for everyone?"

"Yes, thank you," Travis said.

Michelle whispered to Rick, "I can so relate to this… this feeling of never being or doing enough."

Rick grabbed Michelle's hand. "You are enough and do enough. You are more than enough and do more than enough. This journaling is going to help both of us."

Effective Journaling

"Here are three simple steps to get started with journaling, or improve your current journaling process. Choose either a digital or traditional hardcopy format, get the journal if you choose hardcopy, and then simply decide what to write. Let's go into these three decisions a little more thoroughly and then you choose, today, which you'll do."

Clearing his throat, Coach spoke again, "You'll want to decide up front if you want to go with a traditional, physical journal or go digital, such as an online journal, journaling software, or journaling app. Having used both traditional and digital, there are advantages and disadvantages to both formats but it really comes down to your personal preference. Do you prefer to write by hand or would you rather type your daily journal entries? That should make it a relatively simple decision as to which format to use.

"When it comes to a *traditional* journal, while just about anything can work since you're probably going to have it for the rest of your life, there is something to be said about getting a nice, durable journal that you enjoy viewing daily. Get a journal that is not only lined, but also dated, with room to write for every day of the year. I've found that having a pre-designated or dated space to write keeps me accountable to follow through each day, since

I can't help but notice when I miss a day or two, because they're blank. This usually motivates me to go back and mentally review those missed days and catch up my journal entries. It's also nice to have dated journals for every year, so you can easily go back and review any time in your life, and experience those benefits.

"When it comes to a digital journal, there are also many choices available. Again, it really comes down to your preference and which features you want. Just type 'online journal' into Google or 'journal' into the app store, and you'll get a variety of choices," Coach summarized.

"There are infinite aspects of your life that you can journal about, and countless types of journals. Gratitude journals, dream journals, food journals, workout journals, and affirmation and appreciation journals. You can write about your goals, dreams, plans, family, commitments, lessons learned, and anything else that you feel you need to focus on in your life. My journaling method varies. Sometimes it is a very specific, structured process. I journal about things like listing what I'm grateful for, acknowledging my accomplishments, clarifying what areas I want to improve on, and planning which specific actions I'm committed to taking to improve. There are times I just do a dated entry with a synopsis of my day. I find both to be very valuable, and it's nice to mix it up.

"We've included some Scribing Pages in your 30-Day Challenge Fast-Start Kit. Please start by writing your affirmations and we'll cover more the rest of this week. It's your last week in the 30-Day Challenge. In your Journal or Blessings Book, write what it means to you when you hear the phrase, 'Finish Strong.' Go, and we'll see you tomorrow!" concluded Coach.

Rick Becomes a Runner

The morning felt great. Rick turned the first corner and picked up pace. It was exhilarating. He breathed in the cool morning air and floated down the road. He knew he had lost a few pounds, but even more importantly, he felt great. He no longer hated running. Not only had he stopped hating it, he actually looked forward to it - even missed it when he didn't get to run. He felt like a different person than he was a few weeks ago. *I am a runner!*

DAY 30: FINISH STRONG, THIS IS JUST THE BEGINNING!

"We did it!" Michelle announced, lifting her coffee cup. After a day of "observation" and a few tests in the hospital, the doctor signed off on her coming home. She looked good. He could see the pride in her eyes and hear the respect in her voice. *That feels good.*

"We did it. Cheers!" he replied, touching his cup to hers. He smiled. *I did it! I can't believe I got up an hour earlier for 30 straight days! I feel great! My gut is going away! I feel such a sense of accomplishment every morning. Awesome.*

Rick had come to enjoy the mornings with Michelle and the calls with Coach. He'd even connected with quite a few of the others practicing the Miracle Morning 30-Day Challenge in the online community.

Graduation and Commencement

Coach started the call and Rick could hear him take a deep breath. In a voice bursting with pride, he said, "I am so proud of you for completing your Miracle Morning 30-day Challenge! Not all of those who started made it to this point, but you did. Just think how far you've come in just 30 days of doing the Miracle Morning! Many of you have lost weight. Many of you had your best month in your real estate career! And every single one of you has shared feeling happier and more focused than you have at any other time in your life. And that's just in your first 30 days!

"Most of you also told me that you didn't even feel like you were doing the *Life SAVERS* correctly! So imagine how far the Miracle Morning will take you knowing what you know now. As you continue to grow and improve, your ability to accelerate your growth compounds. Imagine where you'll be in 30 days after another round of the 30-Day Challenge. Imagine where you'll be six months from now. Imagine a year from now!

"So, I challenge you. Now that your first 30-day Challenge is over, it's time to start your next one. That's right, I'm suggesting that you start living your life in 30-day Challenges, because there is simply no good reason not to! Now that you've experienced how profoundly the Miracle Morning can transform your life in 30 days, it's time to define the next level, and dedicate the next 30 days to taking yourself there. There will always be a 'next level' for you, and now you have the strategy guaranteed to take you there.

If there is ever anything I can do to support you, you have my phone number and email address and of course, there is *The Miracle Morning Community*, online at **MyTMMCommunity. com**. It is truly the most positive, supportive, and active online community that I have ever seen! I encourage all of you to go there and plug into that group of Miracle Morning practitioners.

Remember, this is only the beginning. You've risen repeatedly, day after day, and now it's your time to shine," Coach said, ending with passion. Rick felt unstoppable, like he could run through a brick wall - and would - for his family.

Learning

After hearing Coach today, Rick and Michelle didn't want to stop their momentum and decided to renew their membership for another 30-Day Challenge. They knew their challenges were not all conquered and they still had very far to go to be all they could be, do all they could do, and have all they could have. They understood a Level 10 Life and perhaps even tasted it at times. But still there was much to learn. *Learning…*

Rick had truly enjoyed learning about self-improvement, high achievement, *Life SAVERS*, the Miracle Morning… and best of all, how he could improve his relationship with Michelle. Life was good, and with a strong morning ritual established and a baby on the way, he could only imagine how great it was about to become.

Until he received the text.

How to Handle a Knife Wound

Rick got to the office and he could tell Vanessa was furious.

"I can't believe Denay and Damion would do this!" she said holding up a postcard.

The postcard essentially stated that Damion and Denay had left Rick's company because they wanted to "provide better service" and "deliver full-service real estate for less cost." It had been sent to every person in Rick's database.

Rick took a deep breath. He was calm. *Where did that come from? Why aren't I furious and throwing things?*

"Let's do a Call Night. Are you available tonight?" Rick asked calmly. "And let's get Jefferson in here as well. I'll ask Michelle if she will help us. I bet she will."

"I'm in! Got it!" Vanessa responded aggressively. "Aren't you angry?"

"I am," Rick replied. "But the meditation in the mornings has taught me to take a moment to calm myself and get centered, so I can gain clarity. I've learned that it's better to take action with a clear head… not throw things or cuss."

"Wow," she said, calmer than before. "Okay. I'll order the food and drink for tonight - and for tomorrow night as well, just in case."

"Excellent," he replied, then added, "Oh, and Vanessa… Thank you. Thank you for being so loyal, so dedicated, and just so… trustworthy."

"Well… wow," she replied. Rick could see she was blushing. "Thank you, for this opportunity. And… and it's good to have you back and… and just well, thank you too."

The 5K

Rick and Jefferson finished the race together, sprinting to the very end. Rick felt great to finish with the younger, thinner Jefferson. He could tell Jefferson was impressed. The run felt great.

As they stretched, Rick reflected on how far he had come in the last 30 days. *What a difference a month can make!*

They decided to grab an early lunch after the run. They slid into opposite sides of the booth.

"Rick, great run, brother," Jefferson said. "You really ran well for…"

Rick laughed. "For an older guy?"

Jefferson chuckled. "Well, yeah."

"Thanks, I think," Rick said. "Well, next time, two weeks from now, I am committed to lowering my time by a minute. You up for that?"

"Oh yeah," replied Jefferson. "And Rick, I just have to tell you how much I appreciate you and the opportunities you've given me. I have four incredible families under contract, and I showed all weekend to three other couples. When these contracts close, I will have earned more than I did all last year."

"You deserve it," Rick replied.

"Well, thank you," Jefferson said, then added, "When I first met you, I didn't know what to expect. I hadn't seen you in the office and it just seemed like you were a ghost. I could tell how angry you were the first day when Damion and Denay left. But if they hadn't left, I would have never had this opportunity. So in a way, I'm glad they left. I'm glad you are my mentor and I believe it's their loss. Big time."

"Thank you, Jefferson," answered Rick. "And thank you for pitching in to help during our Call Night."

"Oh, absolutely," Jefferson chuckled. "Remind me if I ever think about leaving not to worry about the database. That was amazing how your clients rallied around you and how Damion and

Denay's marketing to them actually backfired, making them think of you and how great you were. To get eleven referrals on those calls and more sure to come, was just terrific. The visualization strategy you gave before making those calls was something I will remember forever. And listen to this, guess who gave me a referral today?"

"Who?" Rick replied.

"Lisa, you know, at the front desk?" Jefferson answered. "Lisa gave me, actually me and you, a referral today. Her sister and brother-in-law want to sell and move to a bigger home. How amazing is that? How many agents pass by her every day? I guess there may be something to this affirmations thing. I've been saying 'I am committed to getting referrals from everyone I know today no matter what' every day. And now I'm getting referrals from everyone I know." He chuckled.

Rick chuckled as well. It felt good. Life felt good. "Thank you, Jefferson," he replied. Rick noticed Jefferson had brought a black book with him into the restaurant. "What's that?"

"My journal," Jefferson answered. "You suggested it and I immediately got one - a cheap one. I'll get a more expensive one later, but I can tell this habit is going to stick. I've written in it every day this week. It's even become my 'idea download' place when I have an idea or remember something I should do for a client. It's been really helpful and now I carry it everywhere I go."

Rick laughed, reached into his windbreaker, and tossed a worn red journal onto the table. They both laughed.

Two young ladies approached them. "Hey, we saw you two running at the 5K. We are newer at this running thing. Would you be interested in helping us - and a few of our friends?"

Rick looked at Jefferson and smiled. *A running club? Rick Masters leading a running club?*

— 12 —

DAY 90:
THE EXPONENTIAL GROWTH
SUMMIT

Rick rolled out of bed, drank his large cup of water, went into the bathroom and brushed his teeth. He splashed his face with some cold water and looked into the mirror. Down 20 pounds, his face was thinner, healthier. He felt good. No cartwheels or jumping up and down. But good, solid good. In control, good.

He went to his spot in the spare room, rolled out his mat, and sat cross-legged. He took a deep breath and easily and rapidly got into a comfortable state of quiet. His breathing was regular, deep, without effort, in through the nose, and out through the mouth. To an observer, Rick would look like the epitome of calm. After a few moments, he opened his eyes.

Without getting up, he grabbed his red journal. He wrote his affirmations and included those things he was grateful for, what he called his "appreciations." He took a few minutes to look back at his nearly ninety entries. It was amazing to see the ideas he had, the issues he thought were big then. *Compared to Michelle and the baby, it's all just stuff.* He jotted a few notes.

Rick then closed his eyes and began his visualization. Today's focus, suggested by Jay Michaels, was The Perfect Day. He wrote out his entire workday from Miracle Morning to Bedtime Ritual. He realized that his visualization was so much clearer and felt more natural than when he had begun a couple of months ago. He also realized that it was so much closer to realization - and he could feel this day happening. It wasn't this "dream" any more. It was a vision, pulling him closer to it every day. *Powerful.*

He was still running as part of his Miracle Morning, but he really enjoyed doing some basic yoga moves in the morning. Coach was right; it really was one of the best forms of exercise. He went through a yoga routine. Then he read a few sentences from a spiritual, self-help book. This was the fifth book he had read in the last three months. He did twenty repetitions through what he called his "yoga-pray" routine. *Big improvement from five reps the first day!*

Refreshed. Rejuvenated. Ready.

With a drink of water, he walked confidently into his day. *Let's do this.*

Exponential Growth

The convention center was full. It was full of people and it was full of energy. It was supposed to be a real estate conference, but felt more like a concert. Rick was so excited for the day. He heard the upbeat music playing in the ballroom. He felt a bounce in his step. He stepped through the VIP entrance and onto the red carpet. He knew others were looking at him, but he didn't care. He had eyes for one person. There across the room, he spotted her.

Dressed to the nines, sporting a baby bump, but looking like a princess, was Michelle. He came up behind her, wrapped his arms around her, and kissed her on the cheek.

"Hi beautiful!"

Michelle replied, "Hi honey! Hey, they wanted you to sit in the front row and I get to sit with you. Do you know why?"

Rick just shrugged and said with a smile, "I think they're using me to get to you."

The crowd packed the house. The music wasn't turned off. It was turned up and Reece and Ken clapped their way onto the stage. The entire crowd clapped and stomped along with them.

"Welcome to the Exponential Growth Summit!" Ken announced.

"Whoohoo!" the crowd responded.

"Are you ready to get this party started?" Reece hollered.

"YEAH!" the attendees roared.

"Please have a seat and let's make it happen," Ken said.

"Today, we have a special treat for you!" Reece said after the crowd settled. "Not only do we have one of the hottest speakers in the country with us. We have TWO!" The crowd erupted again.

Reece and Ken started Rod's video. The entire room got dead silent.

"Please welcome Rod Halsten!" Reece said after the video ended. Rod explained the three steps to overcoming mediocrity and living a Level 10 Life.

Rod added, "Let's play devil's advocate for a moment. Can The Miracle Morning really transform your life in just thirty days? I mean, come on… can anything really make that significant of an impact on your life, that quickly? Well, remember that it did for me, even when I was at my lowest point. It has for thousands of others. Ordinary people, just like you and me, becoming extraordinary.

"During The Miracle Morning 30-Day Challenge you'll identify the habits you believe will have the most significant impact on your life, your success, who you want to be and where you want to go.

"When you commit to The 30-Day Challenge, you will be building a foundation for success in every area of your life, for the rest of your life. By waking up each morning and practicing The Miracle Morning, you will begin each day with extraordinary levels of discipline, clarity, and personal development. Thus, in the next 30 days you'll find yourself quickly becoming the person you need to be to create the extraordinary levels of personal, professional, and financial success you truly desire.

"You'll also be transforming The Miracle Morning from a concept that you may be excited and nervous to 'try' into a lifelong habit, one that will continue to develop you into the person you need to be to create the life you've always wanted. You'll begin to fulfill your potential and see results in your life far beyond what you've ever experienced before.

"In addition to developing successful habits, you'll also be developing the mindset you need to improve your life—both internally and externally. By practicing the *Life SAVERS* each day, you'll be experiencing the physical, intellectual, emotional, and spiritual benefits of Silence, Affirmations, Visualization, Exercise, Reading, and Scribing. You'll immediately feel less stressed, more centered, focused, happier and more excited about your life. You'll be generating more energy, clarity and motivation to move towards your highest goals and dreams.

Rod continued, "Remember, your life situation will improve after—but only after—you develop yourself into the person you need to be to improve it. That's exactly what these next thirty days of your life can be—a new beginning, and a new you.

"If you're feeling hesitant, or concerned about whether or not you will be able to follow through with this for thirty days, relax— it's completely normal to feel that way. This is especially true if waking up in the morning is something you've found challenging in the past. It's expected that you would be a bit hesitant or nervous, and it's actually a sign that you're ready to commit, otherwise you wouldn't be nervous.

"It is also important that you take confidence from the thousands of other people who have already gone from living on the wrong side of their potential gap to completely transforming their lives with The Miracle Morning 30-Day Challenge. In fact, you'll hear a few of their stories here in a bit. I really believe the example of others can shine light on what's possible for all of us," Rod concluded.

Reece and Ken returned to the stage. Ken laughed and yelled, "Rod Halsten y'all!"

The crowd erupted again.

Reece let the crowd quiet some and then announced, "Now, let's keep this party going. A real treat for you today. Bestselling author and the father and founder of the Generosity Generation, the largest Global Referral Community in the world, Jay Michaels!"

The crowd stood and gave an Exponential Growth Summit welcome to Jay.

Jay took the stage like he owned it. Rick could see the energy in his step. Jay exclaimed, "Rise and shine agents! Today is your day! He who owns the morning owns the day. It's been said that our quality of life is created by the quality of our habits. If a person is living a successful life, then that person simply has the habits in place that are creating and sustaining their levels of success. On the other hand, if someone is not experiencing the levels of success they want, they simply haven't committed to putting the necessary habits in place, which will create the results they want. It's that simple! Look at your neighbor and say, 'That's simple.'"

Rick and Michelle looked at each other. "That's simple," they said in unison. They laughed. *Michelle is so beautiful when she laughs.*

Jay continued, "Considering that our habits create our life, there is arguably no single skill that is more important for you to master than controlling your habits. You must identify, implement, and maintain the habits necessary for creating the results you want in your life, while learning how to let go of or replace any negative habits which are holding you back from achieving your true potential.

"Habits are behaviors that are repeated regularly and tend to occur subconsciously. Whether you realize it or not, your life has been, and will continue to be, created by your habits. If you don't control your habits, your habits will control you. Unfortunately, if you're like most, you were never taught how to successfully implement and master positive habits. There's no class offered in school called "Habit Mastery." There should be. Such a course would probably be more important to your success and overall quality of life than all of the other courses combined.

"The Miracle Morning gives you the opportunity to master what I would consider one of the most important habits - the habit of the Morning Ritual. Many think the Miracle Morning is about mornings. That couldn't be further from the truth. The Miracle Morning is about self-improvement. It's not about getting up earlier. It's about getting up BETTER! When looking at the habits and techniques of the super-successful, there are commonalities. Meditation, Visualization, Affirmations, Appreciation, Generosity, Exercise, Reading, Journaling… these are the weapons of the super-successful and high achievers in their fight against mediocrity. The age-old issue has been, where and when do we do these?

"Top producers know batching and stacking is the solution. When doing a certain activity, we should attempt to put those types of activities together to maximize efficiency, be in the right frame of mind, and utilize our resources properly. For example, the Networking Stack in *(7L) The Seven Levels of Communication*. The Stack is a grouped set of One-on-Ones. We know One-on-Ones are critical in networking and rather than chaotically or reactively scheduling them throughout the week, we batch them together in the stack. We get the advantages of not having to drive around, introducing key referral sources and networkers between One-on-Ones, and being able to totally focus and listen to our networking partners.

"The same strategy works for self-improvement. If we know Silence, Affirmations, Visualization, Exercise, Reading, and Scribing are the habits we need to develop to become successful, then it makes all the sense in the world to stack them. So the Miracle Morning could have just as easily been the Miracle Night or the Miracle Lunch, and perhaps for some it could be. But for most, the most powerful time - the time you have most control and the time you have the most focus - is going to be mornings.

"The Miracle Morning is the ultimate morning ritual. Enhance your morning ritual with this simple formula - the *Life SAVERS* - and you will soar to new heights. And as always, BE Love, DO Generosity, and HAVE Prosperity. Agents and brokers, welcome to the Generosity Generation!"

Rick and Michelle shot to their feet and joined the crowd in sharing their love for the speaker. Rick leaned over to Michelle and shouted in her ear - he had to shout for her to be able to hear him - "Isn't this an incredible event?!"

"Yeah!" Michelle replied. "But baby is really pushing on my bladder. I'll be right back."

While everyone was standing, she made her way through the aisle and out the back of the room.

"Agents and brokers, Jay Michaels!" Reece yelled. The audience cheered.

Ken then introduced the next guest. "And now, we get to hear from the number one agent in one of the largest cities in America- and she's been number one for years. How does she do it? She never seeks the spotlight and is as humble as they come, but she's here today to share her secret to success. Let's welcome the one and only Kathy to the stage![7]

Kathy quietly but confidently took the mic. The crowd got quiet to hear every word. "Thank you! I'm not sure if it is a secret, but it's my morning ritual. I can't function without my morning ritual. I MUST get up at least an hour before I hear a voice, any voice. I have a ritual that includes SAVERS and of course coffee." Kathy laughed. The crowd laughed with her.

"Morning is the only time of the day for solitude in my schedule, and in that quiet I am able to get some positive self-talk, closed-eye visualization, inspirational or spiritual reading, and light exercise. Out of the S.A.V.E.R.S. method, I most cherish my silence, my exercise, and my quiet reading time. Having a morning ritual has been my secret not just to my professional success but to personal success as well. I love my mornings."

Reese led the standing ovation as Kathy returned to her seat and then introduced another number one agent.

---

[7] All testimonials are based on real accounts from top real estate agents. For more see Endorsements and the Bonus Chapter.

"We have the honor of having two of the country's top agents here today. Our next guest is also number one in a large city. She is known as the luxury expert and she's here today to share her story. Brokers and agents, let's welcome Stephanie!" Reese enthusiastically exclaimed.

Stephanie waved, took the mic, and as she started, the entire room got quiet. Rick could sense the respect the audience had for Kathy and Stephanie.

"Thank you," Stephanie said. "Mornings are incredibly important for me as well. I do the Miracle Morning. I do it in a little different order - silence, followed by reading, then exercise. The workout could last 10-60 minutes depending on the structure of my day. Then I love on my family and pets before starting my business day. I love my silent time, my affirmations, my visualization, my exercise, and my reading. I am a developing journalist. Haven't embraced that as much as I could, but I'm always growing and looking to improve. I love my mornings too and loving my mornings has led to loving my days and loving my days has led to me loving my life. I love my life!"

Michelle returned and leaned over to Rick. She said, "Two powerful women right there! Loved their stories! Maybe one of us could share our story on stage someday." Rick nodded and smiled.

Reece, in his best announcer voice, said, "And now for our third and final testimonial, we have a local top producer who has an incredible story to share. He's soon to be a first-time dad and we all know what a life-changer that can be! Let's give it up for Rick Masters!"

The look of disbelief on Michelle's face made Rick blush. He laughed and kissed her on the top of the head. As he made his way to the front, Rick heard the murmurs and a ripple of chatter filter throughout the crowd. A lone shadow of a figure at the back of the room scurried out of the ballroom. *Damion.* A quote came to Rick's mind: *The best revenge is massive success.*

He smiled and bounded up the steps to the stage. With every step, the cheers got louder, a lot of the crowd knew of his team's struggles and eventual triumphs. It became a standing ovation led by his beaming wife.

Rick's Running Club

Rick looked at the group of twenty or so runners around him. Some new faces today and then there were the familiar faces of Jefferson and the girls who originated the idea of what was now known as The Miracle Morning Running Club.

Suddenly, Rick couldn't believe his eyes. Across the way, a familiar image stepped through the fog and appeared in the dawn.

Rick could tell from the mannerisms. It was Denay.

Rick felt internal turmoil - a mix of anger and wonder. Part of him wanted to confront her. Another part wanted to question her. *Why?* But within him he felt a strange calm. It was a feeling of being "at peace" with everything. It was the state of being that he had practiced every morning for the last few months. *I forgive her.*

She hesitantly made her way to him. He could tell this was difficult for her. She took a deep breath and with head down, quietly asked, "Got a minute, Rick?"

As Denay explained her side about Rick not being there and Damion having a vision, Rick felt empathy. He might have been defensive or even dismissive before, but this morning, he could only seek to understand - and he did understand. She got sold a bill of goods without Rick being there to be the voice of reason. Now that Damion was being investigated by the real estate commission and could possibly lose his real estate license, Denay was leaving Damion's team.

"It's not what I signed up for," she said. "I'm leaving. Everybody's leaving him."

Rick felt a flash of empathy for Damion. *Hmm, where'd that feeling come from?*

— 13 —

DAY 180:
THE ULTIMATE MIRACLE MORNING

The Miracle of Life

Even with one hundred and eighty Miracle Mornings accomplished, Rick and Michelle knew this morning would be different. Michelle's water had broken early in the morning and now they prepared in the birthing room. Rick paced the room like a caged lion. After over a dozen trips back and forth across the room, he was stopped by Michelle.

"Rick," Michelle said gently. "Go for a run. Please. Go. I'll be fine. The doctor said it will be a little while."

"I don't know," Rick replied. "I don't want to miss the birth of our first child!"

"Take your phone. I'll have the doctor text you if there is any change," Michelle reassured him.

"God, I love you," Rick replied.

Michelle looked up from the bed and said, "Rick, I've noticed that you don't use God's or Jesus' name in vain anymore and you haven't cussed in a long time. I love that change in you."

"Thank you, honey," Rick beamed. "I am committed to being a great father and great husband every day no matter what."

"You know, Jay predicted that you would be on stage if you signed up for the 30-Day Challenge," Michelle said.

"What?"

"Yeah, at the Generosity Generation event, he gave me a hug and encouraged me to have you do the 30-Day Challenge. He said, 'It will do Rick some good and there's a lot of good in Rick. I see him sharing his story on stage someday.' He was right. There's a lot of good in you, Rick," Michelle said reflectively.

"Wow, thank you," Rick said softly. He kissed her on top of the head. "Hard to hit the road after you say something like that." He smiled.

She smiled back at him and said, "Honey, go. Don't worry about me. The doctor said it would be a while. We'll text you if we need you."

Rick tied his shoes, gave Michelle a kiss on the forehead, and headed toward the entrance of the hospital.

Running

As soon as Rick's feet hit the pavement, he felt free. Even with the lack of sleep, his legs felt strong, his body felt great, and his lungs breathed in the cool air. *Freedom! Feeling good! I love my life!*

As his strong and lengthy strides ate up the road, his mind was alert and sharp. He reminisced on the last six months.

He thought about how the power of **Silence** had fundamentally changed him. How he had always mistakenly assumed that meditation was some weird, mystical practice. He had never contemplated the importance of quieting his mind and accessing the stillness inside of him. Now he knew that, not only was meditation not weird, but its benefits were deeply rooted in neuroscience. What was at first a difficult skill - as he initially had a hard time relaxing and clearing his mind - was now a part of who he was.

He had also found that the power of Silence was not just for mornings. He took time to clear his mind before making calls, listing appointments, buyers' consultations, interviewing team members, and other appointments. He could now go from overwhelmed to calm in less than five minutes from the techniques he had learned from *The Miracle Morning*. How would having a baby affect his having quiet time? *OMG, I'm having a baby!*

Rick felt the tears well up in his eyes. He chalked it up to the wind in his face and the cool morning. He wiped his hand across his face and picked up the pace.

Rick recalled his **Affirmations**. He could repeat them from memory now. As he went through them one by one, he felt unstoppable. It was a feeling he had grown used to, as reciting his affirmations each morning produced it daily.

Rick was forced to slow down as he neared an intersection. He took the right and noticed that the road opened up in front of him.

The quick break at the intersection and being reminded of his affirmations invigorated him. He continued his mental review of the last one hundred and eighty days. He felt the power of *Visualization*. He felt it, at this very moment. He had visualized looking and feeling like this while he ran. He felt like he was floating. He remembered laboring when he started and visualizing, even with some lack of confidence, a moment like this where he felt light on his feet, breathing easily, and the road passing easily and swiftly below his feet. Like Silence and Affirmations, Rick felt the power of Visualization long after he had finished his Miracle Morning ritual each day.

He used visualization in the morning to see his goals as if they were achieved. To see them manifest over time had taken him from disbelief to using the power of visualization in even more situations. Now, the night before, he visualized his next day, hour-by-hour, and imagined the ideal result for each of those hours. The more he did this, the more his days seemed to be happier and to fit his visualization. Even with disgruntled clients, contentious agents, stressed builders, demeaning developers, and in situations that could have caused animosity or negativity, his visualizing the positive result had helped the meetings become more positive. Right now, he took a moment to visualize the perfect result for the birth of his first child. *Easy and smooth birth for mother and baby, healthy for all. Healthy.*

As for *Exercise*, well, what was left to think about here? He had gone from hating running to forming a running group and enjoying running. He had lost so much weight and even more importantly, his energy level was off the charts. He was happier and his relationship with Michelle was better because of his health. Rick also felt empowered because he had not let Michelle's pregnancy cravings and inability to run derail his desire to run and eat healthier. Michelle wanted root beer, Doritos, Taco Bell, and ice cream - and that was just for lunch! Rick stifled a laugh as he ran. Rick went on those errands for Michelle and had not broken his promise to himself about eating. *I'm a runner. I am committed to eating healthy today and every day, NO MATTER WHAT so I can create and enjoy Level 10 health and energy.*

And **Reading**. Rick had never been a consistent reader. Now, with reading a little bit each morning, he had read five self-improvement books. He now understood what Jay Michaels meant when he said books are the closest thing to a magic pill. To condense all the years of experience, the wisdom, and the secrets of success into a package that can nearly fit in your pocket and costs less than $30… well, that's just amazing. He had already utilized what he learned to hire better people, construct and implement better systems, and leverage technology even more powerfully. He was a better leader. *Readers ARE Leaders.*

Last but certainly not least, was **Scribing**. Writing was not one of Rick's favorite activities until Coach had suggested he write to his yet-to-be-born child. Rick had sporadically written his affirmations and his appreciations, but now his journal was a part of him. It was a written account of his life, each and every day. In it, he captured the greatest lessons he was learning, and recorded the progress he was making. It was something he would one day give to his children, and maybe even pass along to his grandchildren. In fact, he intended on teaching his children the entire S.A.V.E.R.S.

Every day when he left the house, he reminded himself of four things - his keys, his wallet, his phone, and his journal. If he forgot any of these, he felt incomplete. He loved writing his notes and when reviewing it last weekend, he was astounded at not only how far he had come, and how many things he had accomplished, but how much better and more organized his note-taking and writing had become. The word 'scribe' had even become part of his everyday vocabulary. *I love scribing in my journal!*

Rick was jarred out of his thoughts by the vibration of his phone. He stopped. The message made his heart leap. He turned around and started back to the hospital. This time his legs felt like Jell-O, his form was clumsy, and his heart was racing.

Delivery Difficulties

Instead of taking the elevator, Rick tackled the stairs. He ran past his mother and Michelle's parents. He was sweating profusely, breathing heavily, and limping slightly. Brushing past a concerned nurse, he burst into the birthing room.

"What's nuchal mean?" Rick demanded bursting in the room huffing and puffing.

Michelle and the doctor looked at Rick like he was a crazed madman. Rick looked at his reflection in the mirror. He looked like a crazed madman. He caught his breath and gathered himself.

"Rick, it means the umbilical cord is wrapped around the baby's neck," Michelle said. *How can she be so calm?*

Rick looked at Michelle and then at the doctor. *Why do they both look so calm?!*

The doctor reassured him, "Rick, it's not normal, but it isn't unusual either. The baby is breathing through his cord. He's getting blood and air. All is fine. We'll have to be careful just like we always are. We have some time. Why don't you take a shower and relax a bit?"

Relax? How am I supposed to relax?

Rick looked at Michelle. She looked like an angel. She looked like she was okay. He relaxed. He kissed Michelle on the forehead, nodded to the doctor, grabbed his bag of clothes, and headed for the shower.

The Ultimate Miracle Morning

A few hours later, Rick and Michelle were new parents. Thankfully, the delivery went perfectly. The hospital staff was wonderful. Rick coached Michelle through the entire process and

Michelle handled the stress like a pro. It went as Rick and Michelle had visualized.

They hugged each other and their new baby. Rick didn't know if he had ever felt such love. *This is what purpose feels like.*

"If having a baby is like this," Michelle whispered nodding at the bed and looking down at the newborn, "I could do this again." Rick laughed and Michelle smiled a tired smile.

"Wow," Rick replied. "I don't know. We have to get through the first morning first."

"Are you going to do your Miracle Morning today?" Michelle asked quietly.

"Today is all about you," Rick said. "I think I will do a short version. I'll do the 6-Minute Miracle Routine Coach taught us, because I think if I don't, this memorable day just wouldn't feel right. We've come a long way in six months, haven't we?"

"Yeah, thanks to Coach, the 30-Day Challenge, and the Miracle Morning," Michelle said.

Rick hugged his new son and Michelle closer and said, "Perhaps there should be a Miracle Morning for Mothers or Parents…" - they both looked down - "or Kids!?" Rick and Michelle laughed as their newborn slept peacefully. Rick looked at them. The warmth in his heart was overflowing. He knew that this, of all mornings, was a Miracle Morning.

(The End)

BONUS CHAPTER

The Not-So-Obvious Success "Secrets" of Top Real Estate Agents (and How You Can Become One, Too)

Thank you for reading *The Miracle Morning for Real Estate Agents*. We are sure you found the story of Rick and Michelle compelling and inspiring.

But you might be wondering, *"What about me? I'm NOT a morning person. In fact, I'm a night owl. I don't have a lot of extra time to read, exercise, or practice the Life SAVERS. I don't even know how to start or where to begin!"*

Don't worry; you're NOT alone! In fact, *most* of the top 1% achievers interviewed for *The Miracle Morning for Real Estate Agents* said that they were also not morning people prior to reading the book and adopting the Miracle Morning practice. Quite a few of them had never heard of *The Miracle Morning*, and yet they were already engaging in many of the success practices. They also knew they "should" be doing the different activities, but didn't have a structure to do them, and certainly didn't feel like they had the time to fit them in.

Those that had read *The Miracle Morning* were able to soar to new heights of productivity and achievement *because* they took the time to adopt the SAVERS, stick with them past the initial 30-Day Challenge and turn them into a daily habit.

As we spoke to top achiever after top achiever, two common themes appeared:

The first wasn't surprising, at least to us: Every single person had already integrated at least a couple of the SAVERS into their lives and businesses even before reading *The Miracle Morning* … which is, of course, a major part of why they were in the top 1% to begin with.

The second got us really excited: The longer they continued doing the SAVERS, the better the results. Increased revenue, focus and achievement, decreased weight, worry and stress … just to name a few.

Dan Grieb's story, with the Dan Grieb Team (Keller Williams), in Orlando, Florida, is indicative of what we heard over and over:

"My favorite part of The Miracle Morning *practice is the affirmation and reading. The Miracle Morning has given me an organized path to do what I was always told to do. The Miracle Morning put it in a set format that makes sense and has carved out the time for me to do it.*

"Before The Miracle Morning, *I was not a morning person. But, I understood the importance of doing my morning prospecting, and I*

was consistent about doing that. However, I was inconsistent with the affirmations, exercise, reading, and scribing. I was living one fifth of my life by design. I knew that I needed to do the other five things. I simply did not believe I had the time. So for parts of my life, I was very healthy and my business suffered, or I was learning and growing by reading, but my health, vision and business suffered. Now, because of The Miracle Morning, *I get all of the most important items done before I start my day."*

The best part of Dan's story will inspire you to start doing the SAVERS as soon as tomorrow:

"I am down twenty-five pounds since I started doing the SAVERS, and I have another forty to lose. My business in terms of vision is better and I am more productive overall. I have a clear plan to attack each day because I have time every day to see it before it happens. I am more available for my family in the evening because I am not worried about tomorrow. I know I will be up before tomorrow starts, and I can attack it with a clear mind in the morning. The Life SAVERS is a tool, once used, that can change your life. Some people will make excuses others will make it happen. There are a lot of people that have a lot of will power, they just need a clear and direct plan. The Miracle Morning Life SAVERS is that clear and direct plan to get it done."

Lee Gallaher, Gallaher Real Estate in Mulkilteo, Washington, shared his incredible results from just fourteen months of using the *Life SAVERS*:

"For me, the Miracle Morning is, and always has been, very personal. It is not a competition to see how many days in a row I can do or, a "have to" do it. It is a practice that has deepened my life. The compounded effect of my Miracle Morning is something, about which I am very excited. My first year Miracle Morning measurable results: personal income increased of over 29%, my fitness level is 15% better, aliveness, hope and confidence: up 30%. My Miracle Morning practice is constantly evolving. It remains very personal, and I am grateful that it was written."

The Not-So-Obvious Secrets

Additionally, during the course of interviews conducted with two-dozen real estate agent super-achievers, we discovered some "practical secrets" you can use to put yourself in the top achiever category. We think what you'll discover is that these aren't really secrets, they are the lessons learned by the agents who shared them … they just wish they'd learned and implemented them sooner.

Ronnie Matthews, Keller Williams (Spring, Texas) puts it bluntly: "*Everyone always wants to know the trick. There is no secret, no trick. Put the client first, combine honest work with hard work, have patience, live within your means, and realize every single day that you are in business for yourself.*"

Real Estate Super-Achiever Secret #1: *Stay consistently connected.* There is nothing quite as disconcerting as listing your home for sale, only to have the market reject it as you simultaneously experience radio silence from your agent. The solution? Communication. Our top achievers ran the gamut of simply having a weekly email newsletter, to staying in touch via a thoughtfully constructed full-out campaign, and we found many agents are now giving America's #1 closing gift—Cutco—which are personally engraved with the agent's logo and contact information. They shared that staying in close touch with prospective buyers and sellers, clients, previous clients and strong referral sources, and consistently adding value, was absolutely key to their success.

It was also interesting to note that many of our interviewees set boundaries and expectations that worked both for them and their clients right from the start.

Ed Kaminsky, Kaminsky Real Estate (Manhattan Beach, California), shared his thoughts on communication: "*The key to effectively communicating to clients in the real estate business is simple: communicate more often than you think is necessary. The number one complaint of consumers is they never hear from their agent once they have engaged them. It's a huge mistake and very avoidable. You should speak to your clients every week, and for brand new clients every day for the first week."*

Action Items:

- Determine your boundaries when it comes to your business including, how available you are, your expected response time, etc.

- Develop a strong communication program for your clients and connections.

- Keep clients abreast of developments. Call regularly, email weekly, and use technology to create an outstanding client experience without sacrificing personal time and balance.

Real Estate Super-Achiever Secret #2: *Hire a coach, find a mentor, and develop a mastermind group.* This "secret" is widely-known, and yet new and aspiring agents fail to execute it, much to their peril. If you think you can't afford a coach, you can't afford *not* to have a coach! As you are searching for the right coach for you (easily done by connecting with Michael Reese and Jay Kinder, co-authors of this book and founders of NAEA.com or Michael J. Maher, his Certified Referral Coaching, BOOST! Referral Mastery Training, or CATALYST® Program at www.7LSystem.com), you'll need to simultaneously be searching for a strong and successful mentor. A coach will help you develop a plan and strategize your next best moves, while a mentor will share from their wisdom and experience, saving you days or even decades. Reading the book *Think & Grow Rich* (an interviewee favorite) will drive home the importance of the mastermind concept. The magic of the mastermind is multi-faceted: like-minds coming together to strategize and brainstorm can yield ideas and results far beyond those you can achieve on your own.

Top achiever Diane Kink, of the Kink Team in The Woodlands, Texas shared: *"I knew I had to begin with good habits and a schedule, because this business can take you in many different directions. So, I had a coach from day one."*

Monica Reynolds, Heller Real Estate Group (Encinitas, California) says, *"I have weekly accountability sessions with my coach and I attend eight to ten conferences a year because I believe I must always be learning and growing."*

Action Items:

- Hire a coach.

- Find a mentor.

- Develop a mastermind of 3-11 other individuals who are going in your same direction. (Check out Michael's www.TheMastermindCompany.com for more on forming and attending powerful Masterminds and look for his Mega Masterminds in a major city near you).

Real Estate Super-Achiever Secret #3: ***Develop self-confidence and an unstoppable positive attitude.*** Another side benefit of practicing *The Miracle Morning Life SAVERS* is the self-confidence and positive attitude that is the natural result. As our interviewed agents shared critical distinctions made throughout their years, a key one was the self-confidence they developed ... and wished they had developed *much* sooner. You see, once you radiate genuine self-confidence, people are attracted to you as if by magic. Becoming a person who other people love to be around will be a huge boon for your business.

Hal Sweasey, ReMax Del Oro (San Luis Obispo, California), shared: *"Self-confidence and a positive attitude IS the most important aspect. If you don't have a great attitude you will fail. You must review the reason you're doing what you're doing every day. Your attitude doesn't just happen, it has to be cultivated and nurtured like a garden. If you don't tend to the garden then you'll have nothing but weeds. Developing and maintaining a positive attitude is a nonstop process.*

Just like professional athletes or performers who go on hot streaks, then lose confidence. It's a work in process for your whole life. I have doubts all the time. Now I simply don't let them stop me. I've got a coach and support system that's there to push me to be the best I can be…I haven't even scratched the surface of my potential."

Maria Babaev, Douglas Elliman Real Estate (Roslyn Heights, New York), had the disadvantage of being from a foreign country. But with $50 million in transactions during her best year in real estate, she spoke about not leaving attitude to chance. *"Attitude is everything. The right mindset is key to success in our business, and I practice meditation daily to stay focused. But the number one strategy is using affirmations for excelling and having the self-confidence you need. Your self-confidence, or lack of it, is translated immediately to your buyers. You've got to have it, and if you don't have it, you've got to develop it. The right environment is crucial. Having the right people with positive attitudes around me is key to staying on track, and my own state of mind is paramount. You must not allow yourself to be in a destructive environment."*

Action Items:

- Read *Think & Grow Rich*. Memorize the Self-Confidence Formula and repeat it aloud once a day.

- Decide to become unstoppable! Then, do everything you can to reinforce that decision by reading, listening, and surrounding yourself with amazing and positive people that lift you higher.

Real Estate Super-Achiever Secret #4: *Start each year with a plan and work that plan!* If you don't know where you're going, wherever you end up is just fine, right? The agent that reads this book, all the way to the end, is the agent who has high aspirations and wants to do more transactions and make more money year over year. Well, a year over year increase in gross sales and commissions requires a solid plan that is worked on a daily basis. At the very top of our top achievers were the agents and brokers who spent time at the end of each year to consciously and intentionally plan every aspect of their next year, including goal numbers (listings, sales, agents added to their team), and the actions that support those goals and outcomes.

Cindy Carrigan, Five Star Spokane Group with Keller Williams (Spokane, Washington): *"I identify my next year's goals at the end of each year, then create the monthly goals, weekly goals, and daily actions that I will be taking to achieve them."*

Ed Kaminsky weighed in on this important planning he engages in: *"Each year I create a business plan for the year that takes into account all of my numbers. From daily contacts I have to make, appointments I have to set, appointments I have to go on, how many listings I need to take, how many buyers I need to sell, and how many listings that will actually sell. My ratios related to all of those and, of course, my income and closing goals. I break down where each of my deals will come from and create a specific plan on how I will obtain those deals."*

Action Items:

- Design a plan for the next 12 months. (Check into Michael's BOOST! Referral Mastery program to create a Communication Plan www.7LSystem.com)

- Create affirmations that support the realization of your goals and desired outcomes.

- Review your plan twice daily, and say your affirmations as part of your *Life SAVERS* practice.

Real Estate Super-Achiever Secret #5: *Have a daily schedule.* In a perfect world, you would work the traditional eight hours and make in excess of $1 million per year. But the profession you've chosen can quickly take over every waking hour, bleeding first into evenings, then weekends and holidays … while theoretically leaving you with little personal and family time. It's important to develop a schedule that includes work tasks, one that also includes time for yourself, hobbies, and family. Your schedule is entirely up to you, and there are plenty of top achievers who adhere to a strict schedule that provides them with an income in the top 1%, while allowing them to vacation each year, time to regularly pursue hobbies and interests, and even spend time pursuing other financial opportunities!

Justin Potier spends time prior to leaving his office to ensure his next day's schedule is nailed down, and says, *"Your day begins the previous evening."*

Pat Hiban, top-producing real estate agent, bestselling author, and host of the #1 real estate podcast, *Real Estate Rockstars*, takes a hard line when it comes to the pre-conceived notion that agents are at the whim of their clients, and their life is not really their own: *"It's a decision. You decide to have balance, or you decide not to. I have no tolerance for workaholics. If they decide to have a life that sucks because they want to be slaves to other peoples demands all the time, that's certainly their choice. They don't get "it." Like my mentor always taught me, 'Work funds life.' There is a reason we work, and it's not for self-esteem or ego or something other than to get money to paint our life incredible colors through trips, experiences and interesting people outside of work."*

Action Items:

- Decide to be in control of your schedule.

- Develop an ideal daily schedule in Excel and import those non-negotiable appointments into your calendar. (For examples see www.7LBook.com/timeblock or www. JoinGenGen.com).

Real Estate Super-Achiever Secret #6: *Specialize.* Years ago, Honorée Corder, bestselling author of *Vision to Reality*, began living by the philosophy, *"You grow rich in a niche. A specialist always makes more than a generalist."* This applies to real estate just as much as it does to medicine or even the legal and accounting fields. It makes sense that your largest commissions will result from the largest transactions, so you could choose to specialize in the luxury market. Alternatively, you can choose to specialize in one particular neighborhood, zip code, or niche market (such as "doctors new to town") and become known as *the* person who handles that area or those types of transactions.

Hal Sweasey agrees with the strategy of becoming a specialist, *"Be a great listing agent and everything else will fall into place."*

Maria Babaev knows the power of branding and using a tagline: *"My niche is luxury sellers and international buyers. I specialize in helping those buyers and sellers. My tagline is 'Locally Known, Globally Connected,' and I apply this line tag to all my marketing and branding."*

Action Items:

- Pick your specialty.

- Develop a memorable tagline, and use that tagline everywhere.

Real Estate Super-Achiever Secret #7: *Have a great team.* No man or woman is an island, and no successful real estate agent does every single task on both the buy side and sell side without the help of an amazing team. Finding, hiring, training, and growing a solid team will greatly contribute to your success. Without a great team, you'll only go so far.

Jeff Latham, one of the top agents in the country and founder of Jeff Latham Real Estate, has an incredible team that contributes to making his 150+ transactions a year go smoothly and successfully. *"Everyone on my team is a specialist in different parts of the process. We have the following: listing specialist, buyer specialist, client development specialist, transaction coordinator, executive assistant, marketing coordinator, and lead coordinator. Each one of my team members is paramount to my overall success and their success. You have to have the right team members in the right position to truly succeed."*

Justin Potier, Boardwalk Properties (Long Beach, California) delegates with great success: *"I delegate non-income producing activities to my employees and the appropriate team members. This allows me to spend the majority of my time on the items that matter the most: business building opportunities that make us all successful."*

Action Items:

- Hire the right team members and ensure each team member is in the right position.

- Train them and engage in continuous training.

- Delegate, delegate, delegate … and focus on your key revenue generating activities.

Bonus Secret: *"Don't take no for an answer."* ~Justin Potier. Just because someone is not ready to buy or sell now, doesn't mean you shouldn't stay in touch, because you must! This is where Secret #1 comes into play: stay connected until your buyer is ready to buy, or your seller is ready to sell. No just means, "not now" and you have the opportunity to be in the right place at the right time by staying in touch and only hearing "no" as your permission to stay in touch until the time is right.

Now It Is Up to You!

You are no different than the characters in this book, and not really any different from the top achievers we interviewed as the backbone of this book. In fact, the choice is now yours to adopt the *Life SAVERS* as your daily practice, and implement the secrets our top achievers shared so that you can achieve the levels of success you truly want and absolutely deserve.

We've put together some incredible bonuses and provided you with the tools you need to take yourself, and your success, to the next level. **If you haven't already, please be sure to visit our incredible bonuses page www.TMMAgents.com.**

Authors' Note: Every major project contains within it the many, many people who get the job done. We owe a huge thanks to Diane Kink with the Kink Team and Katie Heaney with Cutco Closing Gifts for interviewing more than two dozen top achievers in real estate to learn how they have achieved the top 1% success in real estate, and also how *The Miracle Morning* and *Life SAVERS* have impacted and changed their lives and real estate results for the better.

A Special Invitation from Hal

Fans and readers of *The Miracle Morning* make up an extraordinary community of like-minded individuals who wake up each day dedicated to fulfilling the unlimited potential that is within all of us. As the author of *The Miracle Morning*, it was my desire to create an online space where readers and fans could go to connect, get encouragement, share best practices, support one another, discuss the book, post videos, find an accountability partner, and even swap smoothie recipes and exercise routines.

I honestly had no idea that The Miracle Morning Community would become one of the most inspiring, engaged, and supportive online communities in the world, but it has. I'm blown away by the caliber of our 40,000+ members, which consists of people from all around the globe and is growing daily.

Just go to **www.MyTMMCommunity.com** and request to join The Miracle Morning Community (on Facebook). Here you'll be able to connect with others who are already practicing The Miracle Morning—many of whom have been doing it for years—to get additional support and accelerate your success. I'll be moderating the community and checking in regularly. I look forward to seeing you there!

If you'd like to connect with me personally on social media, follow **@HalElrod** on Twitter and **Facebook.com/YoPalHal** on Facebook. Please feel free to send me a direct message, leave a comment, or ask me a question. I do my best to answer every single one, so let's connect soon!

ABOUT THE AUTHORS

HAL ELROD is on a mission to *Elevate the Consciousness of Humanity, One Morning at a Time*. As one of the highest rated keynote speakers in the America, creator of one of the fastest growing and most engaged online communities in existence and author of one of the highest rated books in the world, *The Miracle Morning*—which has been translated into 27 languages, has over 2,000 five-star Amazon reviews and is practiced daily by over 500,000 people in 70+ countries—he is doing exactly that.

The seed for Hal's life's work was planted at age twenty, when Hal was found dead at the scene of a horrific car accident. Hit head-on by a drunk driver at seventy miles per hour, he broke eleven bones, died for six minutes, and suffered permanent brain damage. After six days in a coma, he woke to face his unimaginable reality—which included being told by doctors that he would never walk again. Defying the logic of doctors and proving that all of us can overcome even seemingly insurmountable adversity to achieve anything we set our minds to, Hal went on to not only walk but to run a 52-mile ultramarathon and become a hall of fame business achiever—all before the age of 30.

Then, in November of 2016, Hal nearly died again. With his kidneys, lungs, and heart of the verge of failing, he was diagnosed with a very rare, very aggressive form of leukemia and given a 30% chance of living. After enduring the most difficult year of his life, Hal is now cancer-free and furthering his mission as the Executive Producer of *The Miracle Morning Movie*.

Most importantly, Hal is beyond grateful to be sharing his life with the woman of his dreams, Ursula Elrod, and their two children in Austin, Texas.

For more information on Hal's keynote speaking, live events, books, the movie and more, visit www.HalElrod.com..

MICHAEL J. MAHER is the #1 International Bestselling Author of *(7L) The Seven Levels of Communication: Go from Relationships to Referrals*, the #1 Real Estate Sales book on Amazon.com and the highest-rated real estate book of all time (with more than 300 Reviews). Like Hal, Michael faced a life-changing experience when his heart flat-lined due to seven blood clots after a surgery. Known for a decade as North America's Most Referred Real Estate Professional, he is the father and founder of The Generosity Generation, the Global Referral Community of the World's Most Referable Professionals. He is also the CEO of **REFERCO**, which franchises large-scale, upscale masterminds around the world and provides support and leverage to those who run referral-based businesses. He is also the proud father of son, Max, and loving husband to wife, Sheri. The family, including a Jack Russell Terrier named Lucky, lives in Atlanta, GA. **For more on Michael's speaking, writing, and coaching, please visit MichaelJMaher.com.**

JAY KINDER was literally born into real estate. His father, Johnny, started in real estate in 1977, the year Jay was born. At age 19, Jay started his real estate career. By age 24, he established himself as a top real estate agent within the Coldwell Banker franchise, ranking #1 in Oklahoma for sales. By age 28, he started an 8-year run ranked in the top 200 agents in the U.S. as noted by the *Wall Street Journal*. In 2010, Jay created his own brand, Jay Kinder Real Estate Experts, to reflect the strategies and philosophies his real estate coaching firm, the **National Association of Expert Advisors (NAEA)** was teaching. As the Co-founder/CEO of the NAEA, Jay is responsible for providing direction and strategies for the Expert Advisors it serves. Today, more than 40,000 agents in the U.S. and Canada consume the products, services and materials provided by the NAEA. **For more information on Jay and the National Association of Expert Advisors, please visit at NAEA.com.**

MICHAEL REESE—After a chance meeting where he re-connected with Jay—made the fateful decision to become a real estate agent in 2002. In just three short years, Mike became a top producer in the Keller Williams system. In addition to ranking in the top 50 for Keller Williams in the U.S., Mike regularly ranked as one of the top agents in the Southwest region for the organization. With his amazing work ethic and Jay's direction, Mike reached $1 million in GCI in half the time it took Jay. A **Co-Founder of the NAEA**, Mike is in charge of Business Development. In this role, he creates strategic alliances with companies that provide programs, services and technology to real estate agents. His efforts have brought some of the top lead generation and conversion programs to the mainstream real estate community in the U.S. and Canada over the last 8 years. **For more information on Michael and the National Association of Expert Advisors, please visit at NAEA.com.**

HONORÉE CORDER is the author of dozens of books, including *You Must Write a Book, The Prosperous Writers* book series, *Like a Boss* book series, *Vision to Reality, Business Dating, The Successful Single Mom* book series, *If Divorce is a Game, These are the Rules,* and *The Divorced Phoenix.* She is also Hal Elrod's business partner in *The Miracle Morning* book series. Honorée coaches business professionals, writers, and aspiring non-fiction authors who want to publish their books to bestseller status, create a platform, and develop multiple streams of income. She also does all sorts of other magical things, and her badassery is legendary. You can find out more at HonoreeCorder.com.

BOOK HAL TO SPEAK!

Book Hal As Your Keynote Speaker and You're Guaranteed to Make Your Event Highly Enjoyable & Unforgettable!

For more than a decade, Hal Elrod has been consistently rated as the #1 Keynote Speaker by meeting planners and attendees. His unique style combines inspiring audiences with his unbelieveable TRUE story, keeping them laughing hysterically with his high energy, stand-up comedy style delivery, and empowering them with actionable strategies to take their RESULTS to the next level.

"Hal received a 9.8 out of 10 from our members. That never happens."
–Entrepreneur Organization (NYC Chapter)

"Hal was the featured keynote speaker for 400 of our top sales performers and executive team. He gave us a plan that was so simple, we had no choice but to put it into action immediately."
–Art Van Furniture

"Bringing Hal in to be the keynote speaker at our annual conference was the best investment we could have made."
–Fidelity National Title

For More Info - Visit www.HalElrod.com

THE MIRACLE MORNING SERIES

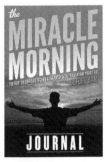

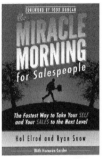

The Journal

for Salespeople

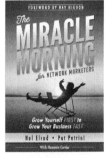

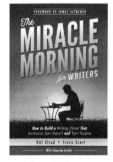

for Real Estate
Agents

for Network
Marketers

for Writers

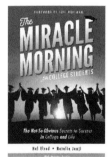

for Entrepreneurs

for Parents &
Families

for College
Students

COMPANION GUIDES & WORKBOOKS

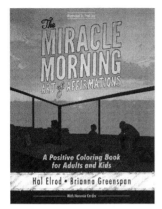

Art of Affirmations

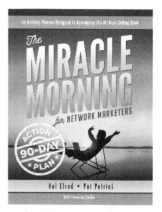

for Network Marketers
90-Day Action Plan

Companion Planner

for Salespeople
Companion Guide

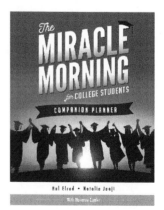

for College Students
Companion Planner